Managing Assertively

Wiley Self-Teaching Guides teach practical skills from accounting to astronomy, management to mathematics. Look for them at your local bookstore.

Other Wiley Self-Teaching Guides on Business Skills:

Accounting: A Self-Teaching Guide, by Neal Margolis and N. Paul Harmon

Effective Meetings: A Self-Teaching Guide, by Clyde W. Burleson

Listening: The Forgotten Skill, A Self-Teaching Guide, by Madelyn Burley-Allen

Making Successful Presentations: A Self-Teaching Guide, by Terry C. Smith

Managing Behavior on the Job: A Self-Teaching Guide, by Paul L. Brown

Quick Business Math: A Self-Teaching Guide, by Steve Slavin

Selling on the Phone: A Self-Teaching Guide, by James Porterfield

Successful Time Management: A Self-Teaching Guide, by Jack D. Ferner

Managing Assertively

How to Improve Your People Skills

A Self-Teaching Guide

Second Edition

Madelyn Burley-Allen

John Wiley & Sons, Inc.

New York • Chichester • Brisbane • Toronto • Singapore

Copyright © 1995 by Madelyn Burley-Allen
Published by John Wiley & Sons, Inc.

Library of Congress Cataloging-in-Publication Data:

Burley-Allen, Madelyn.
    Managing assertively : how to improve your people skills : a self-teaching guide / Madelyn Burley-Allen. — 2nd ed.
      p.   cm.— (Wiley self-teaching guides)
    Includes bibliographical references and index.
    ISBN 0-471-03971-3 (alk. paper)
    1. Supervision of employees.   2. Assertiveness (Psychology).
  I. Title. II. Series
  HF5549.B89 1995
  658.3\02—dc20   94-32607

Contents

Preface

The ideas in this book grew from my own commitment to be effective in my interactions with people. Some years ago, I decided that I wanted to be "in charge of me" in all sorts of situations, many of which are illustrated in this book.

I began by working in improving my listening skills. I started to listen to how I talked with others, and I wasn't pleased with what I heard. I was moved to investigate, learn, and internalize the assertive approach to interacting with others. I would often hear people say, "I'd like to be better at saying no . . . handling criticism . . . stating limits and expectations . . . expressing positive and negative feelings . . . facing stressful situations." Since the assertive approach had helped me in these very same areas, I decided to put together a workshop that focused on these assertive techniques.

Supervisors, of all the people who have the task of managing people, are often given no training in the "people skills" areas of their job. They are usually promoted because they are good hard workers who don't cause trouble, not because they know how to handle or manage others. This book is written for individuals who are committed to improving their people skills.

Although the focus of this book is on helping supervisors and managers be more assertive so they can influence their staff in positive ways, the skills, techniques, and concepts can be applied from any position— parent, peer, teacher, or family member. All of the techniques and most of the concepts can effectively be used in any walk of life. In addition, the concepts and skills in this book are included in a variety of seminars I conduct: How to Deal with Difficult People, Building Self-Esteem, Customer Service, and How to Have Winning Relationships, to name just a few. These seminars were taught in India, China, Singapore, Malaysia, and Indonesia. In other words, this information has universal applications.

Since the first edition of this book was published in 1983, hundreds of organizations are using the material very successfully. The feedback I receive from them includes such statements as: "The participants were fortified with new skills that will make their lives as managers more productive and less stressful," "I feel that the confidence I had when dealing with a difficult and high-risk situation at work was a result of what I learned in the training class," "The evaluations ranked your Managing Assertively class in the top 10 percent of similar STC management classes throughout the state," "The skills received will help me become able to change my attitude and my ability to deal with difficult situations and I learned a variety of techniques that will help me solve some problems I'm having in the office."

The people who made these statements will have a positive impact on those with whom they work and live, that will have a ripple effect. The world changes through the efforts of individual change!

More than likely, some of the phrases used in this book may seem unfamiliar, unnatural, or even contrived. That is because these phrases represent new ways of expressing oneself. It is probably best if you don't read the book all at once. Work through one chapter: experience the resulting new behavior to get the feel of what it means for you; and keep track of your progress as suggested in the book. Internalizing new skills and behaviors takes practice and a belief that you have the choice to do what you want, no matter what. However, those who are persistent in applying the phrases, behaviors, and beliefs contained in this book will experience significant changes. You may find yourself struggling through barriers to reach your goal, but the struggle will be worthwhile.

Special thanks to Ruth Nagler, who provided me with the first opportunity to present my assertive workshop, and to Walt Thompson, Sherry Reson, Lily Sanchez, Frank Graeber, Peggy Dillaman, and the other individuals in a variety of organizations for making it possible for me to conduct numerous workshops over these past two years. Gratitude is extended to each person who has attended my workshops for the part he or she played in assisting me in developing he material contained in this book. Without their input, the examples, ideas, and methods would not be as clear, relevant, and specific to on-the-job situations experienced by individuals having the task of managing others.

My special thanks are also extended to Dianne Littwin for her belief in me; Pam Byers and John Ware for their support and encouragement; Alicia Conklin for her patience and understanding; Karl Weber for his astute comments and suggestions; Judith McCarthy for her assistance in making this second edition happen at John Wiley & Sons; and Dorothy

Sipple, Jeannine Marino, and Judith A. Buchanan for the many hours of typing and for their help in completing the manuscript for this book.

I am grateful most of all to my daughters, Kathleen, Jannice, and Arlene, who were part of my growth and development. Each one had a unique part in my becoming a more assertive and loving mother. What I learned through my relationships with my daughters allowed me to have enhanced relationships with my three grandchildren, Dana, Erika, and Christopher. They, too, had their influence, but in a different way. My family relationships gave me many opportunities to learn lessons and practice my assertive skills.

Madelyn Burley-Allen

For more information about the Creative Self-Assertion Profile and Managing Assertively Workshops conducted by Madelyn Burley-Allen, contact:

Dynamics of Human Behavior
P.O. Box 2344
Wimberley, Texas 78676
Phone: (512) 847-0595
Toll free: (888) 516-9575
Fax: (512) 847-0597
Email: dhb8@wimberley-tx.com
Web: www.dynamics-hb.com

1   **The Gateway to Effectiveness**

What are the most common complaints of workers about their bosses? In a survey* of several thousand employees, the top nine were:

- Arbitrariness
- Arrogance
- Failure to show appreciation or give credit
- Failure to see the other person's point of view

---

*What Every Supervisor Should Know, by Lester R. Bittel (New York: McGraw-Hill, 1974), p. 21.

- Lack of leadership

- Lack of frankness and sincerity

- Failure to delegate responsibility

- Indecisiveness

- Bias; letting emotions rule reason

Perhaps you are a boss who is reading this book with the hope that you do not have and will never have that kind of negative image.

My intent throughout this book is to show how managing others assertively, as well as managing yourself assertively, can be a way to avoid behaviors that result in ineffectiveness. We will explore what you can do to develop your managing skills and what methods you can use for effectively handling others with success. My goal is to ensure that the nine most common complaints won't be directed at you.

Although the nine complaints were directed at people's bosses, seven of the nine, and perhaps all nine, could be said of anyone in any relationship. The two complaints about which I have reservations are lack of leadership and failure to delegate responsibility. However, in our personal lives—with family, friends, community groups, and social organizations, we often assume a leadership role and certainly delegate tasks, errands, and responsibility to others. So it is important to apply these skills in all aspects of your life.

DEFINITION AND GOALS OF MANAGING ASSERTIVELY

Definition   Managing others and yourself assertively is based on valuing the uniqueness of each individual. It is defined as follows:

> Managing others and yourself assertively is an approach based on the Seven Keys of Goodness: (1) influencing others in a positive way that encourages people to realize their potential; (2) practicing an active and initiating (rather than reacting) mode of behavior; (3) taking a caring position, emphasizing the positive nature of self and others; (4) exhibiting self-expression though which one stands up for his or her basic rights without denying the rights of others and without experiencing undue anxiety or guilt; (5) possessing a nonjudgmental attitude that diminishes the use of labels, stereotypes, and prejudices; (6) taking responsibility for oneself by not making other people responsible for who we are, what we do, and how we think and feel; and (7) communicating wants, dislikes, and feelings in a clear, direct manner without threatening or attacking.

Goals

The overall goals of managing assertively are to increase your confidence, professionalism, ability to deal effectively with people problems in all aspects of your life and by enhancing your skill to express yourself without violating your own rights or others.

A supervisor gains respect through honest, clear, direct self-expression—the assertive approach to communication. When you communicate in this honest, direct manner, employees soon learn to trust you when you say something can or cannot be done. Assertive communication also includes finding ways to leave the door open, recognizing that there are more ways to deal with problems than an either/or approach might suggest. Managing others and yourself assertively can help you overcome blocks that stop you from being assertive, and so can:

- Increase your effectiveness at handling conflict and criticism

- Help you examine how your conditioning and your past experiences have contributed to your being nonassertive

- Encourage a positive dialogue so that difficult issues can be solved successfully

- Assist you in examining outmoded strategies that could be decreasing your effectiveness

- Provide you with a systematic approach to having a positive influence on others, and

- Increase your potential for career advancement

EXERCISE 1.1

To find out what your managing style is like and to clarify your goals as a supervisor, complete the following self-evaluation exercise. It will aid you in pinpointing those aspects of yourself that you want to improve and those for which you want to take credit for already doing successfully.

Examine the following statements. For each, put an X under either Yes or No.

Assertiveness Assessment

Yes	No	
_____	_____	1. When an unpleasant assignment comes along, is your first impulse to handle it yourself rather than give it to an employee?
_____	_____	2. Do you sometimes feel that your workers take advantage of your good nature?

Yes	No		
_____	_____	3.	Do you refuse unreasonable requests by your employees?
_____	_____	4.	Do you feel guilty when you have to turn down an employee's request for extra time off—even when your decision is justified?
_____	_____	5.	Do you agonize over turning in a poor evaluation of one of your employees?
_____	_____	6.	Do you insist on helping those who don't want your help?
_____	_____	7.	Are you reluctant to speak with an employee who is violating the rules?
_____	_____	8.	Are you able to say no to your boss when he/she asks you to take an action with which you disagree?
_____	_____	9.	Do you find it hard to say thanks and show appreciation to your employees?
_____	_____	10.	Do you have confidence in your judgment?
_____	_____	11.	Do you continue to pursue an argument with an employee after your point has been made?
_____	_____	12.	Are you reluctant to state your feelings when someone is disrupting your staff?
_____	_____	13.	Do you return work to an employee when the work is incorrectly done?
_____	_____	14.	Do you control meetings so that others don't have much opportunity to express their ideas?

Discussion of Exercise 1.1

Now review your responses and determine the ones with which you are dissatisfied. Suppose, for example, you find that you are dissatisfied with number 7, which deals with your ability to enforce company rules.

CASE   Diane, a customer service supervisor, feels that when employees violate rules, she wants to put off any confrontation to another day. She says to herself, "I'll wait until the next time it happens." She doubts her understanding of the rules and her ability to enforce them. She knows that she is not firm enough but is afraid to do something about it.

On the other hand, you may have said Yes to number 14, which deals with how to control meetings.

CASE   Richard, a supervisor in a telecommunications company, finds that his employees are complaining to the manager about Richard's "dictatorial attitude." In his eagerness to make meetings successful, Richard assumes center stage without realizing that other people cannot contribute what they want to say and thus are feeling resentful. He senses that he is coming on too strong, but he isn't sure how to be more sensitive to his employees' needs without becoming ineffectual.

Both Diane and Richard need to modify their behavior so that they can assert themselves effectively. Like Diane and Richard, if you find through this assessment analysis that any of your responses show nonassertiveness, it would be useful to modify your behavior. The important issue here is your willingness to examine your behavior in terms of how you carry out these people-oriented tasks that result in your managing others in an effective or ineffective manner.

EXERCISE 1.2

Examine your yes and no answers on the Assertiveness Assessment. Determine which of those behaviors you want to modify or improve. Then complete the following exercise. This will aid you in defining what you want to accomplish, that is, in setting your goals.

Goal Setting

1. In the area of assertion, I want to:

2. In the area of work, I want to accomplish the following through assertion:

3. I will know I have accomplished my goals when I:

4. My modified behavior(s) will be:

THE JOB OF A SUPERVISOR

It is often the tendency of those who manage others to merely "do what comes naturally." In some cases, this has worked out satisfactorily. However, your success as a supervisor depends heavily on how well you apply direct-supervision skills. The gateway to effectiveness lies in your ability to understand yourself and others, to communicate successfully, to get the job done, and to handle problems in a way that encourages employees to work in a cooperative manner.

The first-line supervisor represents one of the most important forces in the U.S. economy. As a supervisor, you play a major role in the overall success of your organization. You are a leader, a planner of work, a source of technical know-how, and a mediator between policy-setting management on the one hand and rank-and-file workers on the other.

A supervisor is not a manager. The following comparison of functions will assist you in better understanding how your job differs from that of a manager.

Manager	Supervisor
• Sets goals	• Meets the goals
• Plans	• Implements the plan
• Does not schedule others' work	• Schedules workers
• Anticipates problems	• Solves problems as they occur
• Plans the staffing of supervisory positions	• Hires workers as needed
• Knows all relevant functional areas	• Knows his or her own area
• Cannot replace an absent staff member	• Can replace an absent worker
• Delegates training	• Trains
• Finds new resources	• Distributes the resources
• Represents the company	• Represents the workers and the company
• Needs information from company executives	• Needs information from his or her immediate superior
• Spends time with peers in other departments	• Stays in his or her own department
• Meets people outside the organization	• Does not meet people outside the organization

- Mediates and negotiates at organizational levels

- Mediates and negotiates at the unit level

- Has ceremonial duties, such as speeches, and is involved in community affairs

- Has no ceremonial duties

As part of the supervisory training I (the author) do, I have supervisors identify which of the listed functions they perform on the job. A large percentage of supervisors perform both managerial and supervisory functions. It is important for you to acknowledge if this is true for you. It is especially critical if you have plans to move into management. It can help you determine what academic courses to take or other training to seek that will fill the management areas in which you don't have expertise. I've often found that when supervisors are not aware of their skills and the functions they already perform, they might feel they are not qualified to apply for management positions. It is imperative to examine how you carry out these functions because this will determine how successful you will be.

The effectiveness of your work group depends largely on you and your style of supervising. Since your main tasks are directing and controlling, your success will be determined by the approach you use, the way you communicate, the way you approach problems and ask questions, and your attitudes and beliefs concerning those you supervise. Each of these factors will influence your success or failure as a supervisor.

HOW BELIEFS AFFECT YOUR SUPERVISORY STYLE

The chart shown in Figure 1.1 gives you a visual picture of the importance of your beliefs in relation to your supervisory style. Behind every decision you make and every action you take there are beliefs about human nature and human behavior. Many of these beliefs were formulated in early childhood as part of your conditioning. A significant aspect of this conditioning process is the development of the self-concept. Your self-concept includes your ideas of how a supervisor should carry out his or her role. One of the tasks of a supervisor is to find out how his or her self-concept may interfere with the ability to handle employees in a positive way.

An example of one of the major barriers to effective supervision is the belief "I shouldn't supervise in such a way that others won't like me"—

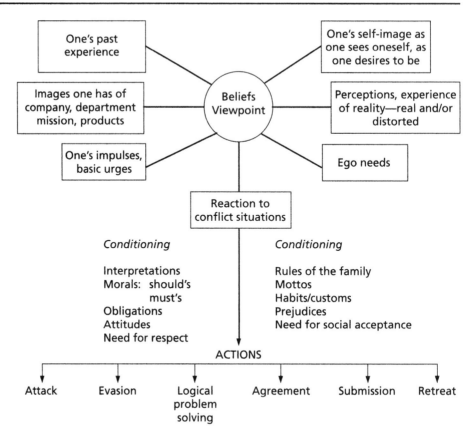

FIGURE 1.1

Influencing factors on human behavior.

Adapted from *The Supervisor and the Job*, by Aaron Sartain and Alton W. Baker (New York: McGraw-Hill, 1978).

an overly strong concern about being liked by employees. This belief is often formulated while a person is an employee. When entering the workforce, employees are encouraged to be friendly and obliging. They are reinforced for sidestepping conflicts and not ruffling anyone's feathers. The reward for such "nice" employees is often a promotion to a supervisory position. This is where the trouble begins.

Their role in the system has now changed. Instead of avoiding personal conflicts, supervisors are expected to confront and solve them. Instead of dodging controversial decisions, they are expected to face up to them. Whereas previously the system manipulated them into being "people pleasers," they are now asked *not* to try to do things to please others. This turnaround results in unhappy supervisors; feelings of guilt, anger, and frustration; and in some cases, ulcers, heart attacks, or alcoholism. Another result is that the organization is hindered by inefficiency, indecision, stagnation, inaccurate performance appraisals, and excessive employee turnover.

CASE Dennis, a sales supervisor, is overly concerned about hurting others' feelings. He is afraid of what others will say and that they won't like him. He often waits for the "right" or "proper" time to confront his employees. He says to himself, "If I ignore it, it will go away." To his dismay, it often doesn't. As a consequence, he frequently faces crisis situations. The employees do indeed like him, but, although he is warm and friendly, he lacks effective leadership qualities.

This type of supervision not only fails to get the job done but also leaves both supervisor and employees frustrated and tense.

Here is another example of how beliefs influence supervisory style.

CASE Jo has the belief that "people's feelings aren't important; it's getting the job done that counts." She often gets the short-term results, but the climate in her department is one of resentment and resistance. Jo is seen as fault-finding and intimidating. In describing her behavior, Mary says, "Jo is so aggressive and critical I feel I can't do anything right in her eyes. I do exactly what she tells me to do, but she is never satisfied. If a problem comes up that might require more work from me, I'll be damned if I'm going to let her know about it!"

This style of supervising may get the basic job done, but it doesn't get much cooperation or involvement from employees.

TWO SETS OF ASSUMPTIONS ABOUT PEOPLE

As the previous case examples show, beliefs play a major role in determining your supervisory style.

In 1954, Dr. Douglas McGregor did a systematic examination of many common but inconsistent assumptions about what makes a manager. His book, *The Human Side of Enterprise,** grew out of these studies. He discovered through his research that the assumptions supervisors hold about controlling their employees determine the character of their unit.

EXERCISE 1.3

Under which of McGregor's two theories do you operate? Before you answer, complete the following survey. It will help you recognize your basic assumptions about human nature as they affect your supervisory style.

*New York: McGraw-Hill, 1960.

Survey of Supervisory Style*

Beside each statement, place an X in the column that most accurately describes the way you function as a manager or how you feel about managing. Be sure to make one choice for each of the statements listed.

	Usually	Often	Sometimes	Seldom
1. Since I carry the responsibility, I expect my subordinates to accept my decisions.				
2. I encourage my employees to meet on their own and to take independent action on job-related matters.				
3. I monitor my subordinates every day or so to see if they are doing the work as assigned.				
4. I believe that my subordinates must be given the opportunity to make mistakes.				
5. I make sure that my subordinates' major workload is planned for them.				
6. My subordinates show self-control and self-direction and are not heavily dependent on me for supervision.				
7. I supervise my subordinates closely in order to get better work output from them.				
8. Employees want to assume more responsibility and should be given the opportunity.				
9. I rely on the authority of my position to get my subordinates to do things.				
10. My subordinates regard me more as a coach and a helper than as a boss.				
11. I have to step in and do the work when I see that an employee isn't getting the job done on time.				
12. I stand behind my subordinates when they make decisions on their own.				
13. I set up controls and lean on people when necessary to assure that my subordinates get the job done.				
14. My people know what is expected and require little direction from me.				
15. I provide my subordinates with activities that will help me to meet my goals and standards.				
16. If I am absent for several days, my employees go about their work just as if I were there.				
17. It's important to get an employee's goals in writing and signed so there is no misunderstanding later.				

*Reproduced by permission of Training House, Inc., Box 3090, Princeton, NJ 08540. Originally published as a four-page self-assessment.

	Usually	Often	Sometimes	Seldom
18. When I give assignments, I let my employees know that I'm sure they can do a good job.				
19. When employees fail to do what they are supposed to do, there is a need for better controls and discipline.				
20. Employees who know what is expected of them will give their best effort and not just try to get by.				
21. Getting the work done correctly and on schedule must take priority over the personal needs of workers.				
22. To be a good supervisor, I take a strong interest in each employee—family, hobbies, goals, etc.				
23. Coffee breaks and lunch periods must be controlled or they result in lost time and productivity.				
24. People want to work. Even if they didn't need the money, people would work.				
25. Employees are interested in what is expected of them rather than knowing management's reasons why.				
26. I believe in spending a lot of time with employees—getting their views and building them into my decisions.				
27. Most employees want to be led. They are dependent by nature and need to be told what to do and how to do it.				
28. Employees who are encouraged to set their own goals will set them higher than their bosses would have.				
29. Unsupervised employees will tend to slack off and not work as hard as when they are being watched.				
30. If you treat employees like kids, they'll behave that way. But treat them like adults, and they'll behave like adults.				

Score Your Survey

1. Place the number 3 over every X in the Usually column.

Place the number 2 over every X in the Often column.

Place the number 1 over every X in the Sometimes column.

Place the number 0 over every X in the Seldom column.

2. Circle the score of each odd-numbered item (1, 3, 5, . . .). Then add all the circled scores. This total represents your theory X score.

Enter your theory X score here: _____

3. Now add the scores of all the even-numbered items, that is, all the uncircled numbers. This total represents your theory Y score.

Enter your theory Y score here: _____

A high score on the theory X line indicates that you believe people tend to be lazy and dependent, preferring security to other rewards. Furthermore, a high theory X score would indicate that you feel people need direction, do not want to think for themselves, and generally need to be shown, told, and closely supervised.

A high score on the theory Y line, on the other hand, indicates that you believe people are naturally active, enjoy setting goals, and aspire to independence, self-fulfillment, and responsibility. Furthermore, a person who scores high on the theory Y side assumes that people who care about and understand what they are doing can devise and improve their own methods of doing work. They need to be respected and are capable of assuming responsibility and self-correction.

Since there are 15 items that relate to your theory X score and 15 that relate to your theory Y score, the highest score in either dimension is 45. A score of 30 or more on either scale suggest that you work from that set of assumptions. If the difference between your X and Y scores is less than 10 points, you have a well-balanced approach to management. You probably respond flexibly to a variety of situations. If the difference between your X and Y scores is more than 10 points, you probably feel at home in one type of environment and uncomfortable in the other.

The assertive supervisory approach promotes the well-balanced approach to management, since the situation and the people involved dictate which method would give the best result. As you will learn in Chapter 3, the theory X style is characteristic of the aggressive mode, the theory Y style of the assertive mode.

On page 13 are the two sets of assumptions that McGregor found most prevalent in the companies he studied. McGregor labeled them "theory X" and "theory Y."

BENEFITS OF LEARNING THE ASSERTIVE APPROACH

Supervision implies endless attention to the behavior of others and requires the most delicate sort of guidance. Supervisors who concern themselves with learning ways to increase their job skills will experience less

ASSUMPTIONS OF THEORY X AND THEORY Y*

	Theory X	Theory Y
Human Nature	People are naturally lazy . . . they prefer to do nothing . . . people remain children grown larger . . . they are naturally dependent on others to lead and to reward or punish them. . . people have little concern beyond their immediate material interests . . . people naturally resist change . . . they prefer the security of the status quo.	People are naturally active . . . they set goals and enjoy striving . . . people normally mature beyond childhood . . . they aspire to independence, self-fulfillment, responsibility . . . people seek to give meaning to their lives by identifying with nations, communities, churches, unions, companies, causes. . . people naturally tire of routine and enjoy new experiences and opportunities for growth.
Training and Development	People need to be told, shown, and trained in popular methods of work . . . people need specific instructions on what to do and how to do it . . . larger policy issues do not concern them. . . people are formed by heredity, childhood, and youth . . . as adults they remain static . . . old dogs don't learn new tricks.	People who understand and care about what they are doing can devise and improve their own methods of doing work . . . people need to see the big picture and to know the why behind their work . . . they constantly grow . . . it is never too late to learn . . . they enjoy learning and increasing their knowledge and skills.
Supervision and Leadership	People expect to depend on direction from above . . . they do not want to think for themselves . . . people need supervisors who will watch them closely, praise their good work, and reprimand errors.	People close to the situation see and feel what is needed and are capable of self-direction . . . people need to be respected and treated as capable of assuming responsibility and self-correction.
Motivation and Rewards	Work is dissatisfying . . . people need money and status rewards to get them to work . . . the main force keeping people productive in their work is fear of being demoted or fired . . . people need to be inspired, pushed, or driven.	Work offers many satisfactions: pride in achievement, social contacts, new challenges, growth . . . the main force keeping people productive in their work is a desire to achieve their personal and social goals . . . people need to be released, given an area of freedom.
Work and Jobs	Jobs come first . . . people are selected, trained, and fitted to meet the needs of the job . . . people are naturally compartmentalized. . . work demands are entirely different from leisure activities.	People come first . . . workers seek self-realization . . . jobs must be designed, modified, and fitted to people . . . people are naturally integrated . . . when work and play are too sharply separated, both suffer.

* From *Styles of Management*, by Dr. Scott D. Parry (Princeton, NJ: Training House, Inc., 1978).

conflict, stress, and frustration. The information in this book will provide you with a framework within which you can work for better understanding of human relations, interpersonal communications, supervisory practices, and alternative ways of solving problems.

Managing assertively can help supervisors with all sorts of problems: Tom, the supervisor of an office staff, wants to learn how to be more effective with his older employees; Joan, a data programmer supervisor, wants to approach her boss concerning his way of pointing out her mistakes; David, factory foreman, is concerned about the best way to deal with an employee's tardiness when a union is involved; Debbie wants to know how to ask her manager for the necessary support to get the training she needs; Jim, head of a finance department, wants to learn to give instructions so that they are carried out; Ken thinks that his employees can be more motivated and is looking for an approach to help him communicate more effectively with them; Mary Ellen, a supervisor of nursing, isn't sure what to do about an employee who often complains about her work assignments; and Doris, a supervisor of a government agency, is told that she comes on too strong and wants to find a more appropriate way to talk about her negative feelings. Each of these problems can be handled though assertive management.

SUMMARY

The goal of managing assertively is to reduce the complaints of workers about their bosses: arbitrariness, arrogance, failure to show appreciation or give credit, failure to see the other person's point of view, failure to evaluate employees correctly, lack of leadership, lack of frankness and sincerity, failure to delegate responsibility, indecision, and bias. This is done by carrying out the Seven Keys to Goodness. As you make more and more of those behaviors part of your personality and put them into practice in your daily life, you will experience more joy and be more successful.

This will increase your supervisory effectiveness—your ability to understand yourself and others, to communicate successfully, to get the job done, and to handle problems in a way that encourages employees to work in a cooperative manner.

A supervisor's style is largely determined by his or her beliefs and self-image, which influence attitudes and help determine whether the supervisor uses the theory X or theory Y style of supervision.

The purposes of managing assertively are to help you:

- Learn ways to stick to the point in a discussion without becoming angry or anxious.

- Work productively with others to a build cooperation and team work

- Confront problems effectively instead of putting them off

- Acquire respect from others while building your self-confidence

- Be aware that each person with whom you work is unique

- Understand that the situation, the task at hand, your personality, and the personality of the other is what determines how to handle a specific problem

2 Building Blocks to Managing Assertively

Many times a day I realize how much my outer and inner life is built upon the labors of my fellow human beings, both living and dead, and how earnestly I must exert myself in order to give in return as much as I have received.
Albert Einstein

We've all had experiences with various kinds of bosses. No doubt two or three of them stand out as individuals for whom you not only enjoyed working but for whom you would go out of your way to get the job done. On the other hand, you probably have had other bosses who stand out because they created a heavy, negative environment that influenced people to feel miserable.

Most, if not all, people would much prefer to be a boss who creates a positive, enjoyable environment. Thus, there is value in taking a moment to reflect on the kinds of bosses you've had to provide you with a clearer understanding of what qualities these bosses had that are similar to or different from your own.

| **EXERCISE 2.1** | **Best and Worst Boss Exercise** |

1. List five behaviors, characteristics, or adjectives that describe the best boss you ever had.

   1.
   2.
   3.
   4.
   5.

2. Now, list five behaviors, characteristics, or adjectives that describe the worst boss you ever had.

   1.
   2.
   3.
   4.
   5.

3. Examine your descriptions of these two people. What is the major difference between them?

4. What qualities of the best boss do you have?

5. What qualities of the worst boss do you have?

6. What action could you take to modify one worst-boss quality in a positive way?

Being "the best boss" is a real challenge! It is to be hoped that, by putting to work the building blocks to managing assertively that are dealt with in this book, you will be closer to that goal. Figure 2.1 shows the

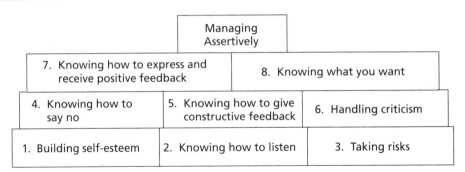

FIGURE 2.1

The eight building blocks to assertive management.

eight building blocks. Each will be explained in this chapter and dealt with in more detail in the following chapters.

BUILDING SELF-ESTEEM

In Chapter 1, the importance of your self-concept and of your perception of yourself as an adult was pointed out. Most often, children are raised to believe that modesty is a great virtue and that pride and boasting should be avoided at all costs. The usual result is that many supervisors have trouble accepting compliments about the work they do and taking credit for their accomplishments.

CASE

Nancy, a supervisor in a retail store, believes that it is wrong to accept positive feedback. She is an excellent supervisor; however, you often hear her say "Anybody could have done that" when complimented on her work. She often discounts positive feedback by saying such things as, "They did most of the work; besides, I make a lot of mistakes."

The disadvantage of this kind of behavior is that it interferes with Nancy's seeing herself in a positive manner. A way to nourish self is to allow yourself to feel satisfied when you function at your best and to acknowledge your strengths and abilities. It is harder to see the best in others when you don't see the best in yourself. Promotion, recognition, and power often go to the people who are self-confident. Modesty can work against you when you are selling yourself to others.

On the other hand, an inflated self-image or a boastfully aggressive self-portrayal can be as damaging as excessive modesty.

CASE   Henry is at the opposite extreme from Nancy. He constantly fishes for compliments. He often makes positive statements about himself while putting someone else down. His constant boasting puts people off, which results in their not wanting to work with him.

Understanding the importance of self-esteem is one of the most essential building blocks to assertive supervision. Later chapters will cover in more detail the elements of how your past presently influences you and the methods you can apply to be more aware of the beliefs that determine how you behave.

EXERCISE 2.2

Which supervisor would most likely be assigned the responsibility for new employees?

A. "I think I can handle four new clerks in our unit. The six I have now are well trained, experienced, and functioning at standard or above. Ann and Carol will be able to assist me in training the new workers."
B. "Oh, sure. I can handle four more. No problem. Just send them along."
C. "Well, I may be able to handle four more clerks. I'm not sure. I do get bogged down sometimes, but I guess I can fit them in."

Answer: Supervisor A, who made a specific, thoughtful, and clear statement of what can be done in terms of the already existing work force, whereas B is too flippant, and C is too hesitant.

EXERCISE 2.3

1. List five of your strengths and abilities.

2. What is your usual response when someone compliments you?

3. Do you want to modify how you respond to compliments? If so, describe the new behavior here.

KNOWING HOW TO LISTEN

One of the most troublesome communication problems in the workplace is the lack of effective listening skills. Assertive supervisors listen to the needs, ideas, and feelings of those with whom they work. When someone is talking, it's easy to spend the time thinking about how you will respond rather than listening to what is being said. Information gets distorted and misinterpreted, which results in misunderstanding and frustration. The temptation is to jump in and tell the person what to do rather than hearing him or her out before you really understand the situation.

CASE June, a systems analyst, went to her supervisor to talk about the new accounting program that she was developing. Her group had already made a number of attempts to solve a particular problem. June had some other alternatives that she wanted to explore, but June's supervisor, who prided herself on her helpfulness, quickly suggested ways to solve the problem. June found herself unable to explain what the group had already tried. When her supervisor ignored her attempts to explain, June simply nodded, listened half-heartedly to her supervisor's suggestions, and left feeling annoyed.

When a supervisor responds to employees by telling them how wrong they are, by attempting to persuade them of his or her own point of view, or by offering reasons why they aren't right, people feel misunderstood and discounted.

The assertive supervisor may not agree with the other's point of view, but he or she gives the person respectful attention and asks thoughtful questions, leaving the person feeling that the supervisor is willing to listen. Poor listening habits force others to repeat the same information over and over. Employees often respond to supervisors who listen poorly by telling them less and less. If a supervisor has a blind spot about his or her willingness to be open and available to the staff, the supervisor may be puzzled by the failure of the employees to come forward for assistance.

CASE Joe, the director of a nonprofit agency, prides himself on his open-door policy. He tells his staff he is always available to listen to problems or hear requests. He can't understand why so few of his staff make use of his open-door policy. He is unable to see that his aggressive, blaming stance makes his staff reluctant to come to him for help.

Failure to listen leads to many kinds of communication problems:

- People acting on what they thought was said rather than on what was really said

- Agreeing to ideas that weren't truly understood

- Completing tasks incorrectly because one doesn't want to seem stupid by admitting that he or she didn't listen

- Misinterpreting the job assignment and, therefore, doing it incorrectly

Just sitting with your mouth closed and nodding your head does not constitute effective listening. Unless you make some kind of response, employees have no way of checking whether you have heard them correctly. Saying nothing usually forces others to guess whether they have been understood or not. Good listening includes indicating your understanding to the other person.

Good listening also requires that you listen with your eyes and your other senses as well as your ears. Suppose someone with whom you are talking is looking at his or her watch every few minutes. It may be important to respond to the message being sent visually. A good listener might say something like, "I notice you keep looking at your watch. I wonder if this is the best time for us to talk."

Managing assertively includes listening to what people say and to how they say it, as well as letting others know that you are listening.

EXERCISE 2.4

Which response indicates effective listening?
A. Jeri nods and rarely says anything when others talk to her.
B. Mitch feels that it is important that his employees understand the "right" way to do things. Therefore, he has a ready answer to any question or comment.
C. Susan will often summarize the ideas presented by an employee to see whether she understands before she responds.

Answer: C. When actively listening, you check your perceptions to make sure you are listening correctly and to let the other person know you heard. Making no response or answering too quickly can turn off the talker.

EXERCISE 2.5

1. Think of someone you know who doesn't seem to listen to you. What does this person do that lets you know that he or she isn't listening to you?

   How do you feel when talking to this person?

2. Think of a person who listens to you well. What do they do?

   How do you feel when talking to this person?

3. Think of a time recently when you didn't listen effectively. What happened?

TAKING RISKS

Risk-taking is one of the major areas where people seem to have difficulty asserting themselves. The risks you take fall into the following categories: speaking up for what you believe, asking for what you want, stating your limits, and expressing your expectations of others. These actions involve risk because people have the mistaken belief that others will respond to them negatively and that they will be judged in an adverse way. People are led to believe that asking for what they want is not OK; and, therefore, doing so is scary. As a result, expressing oneself in this manner entails a certain amount of risk.

Some supervisors have beliefs like these: "Any good worker will know what's required of her without my having to talk to her" and "If he had any brains, he would know I don't like it when he comes in five minutes late." These supervisors believe that others should understand what is wanted without any explanations. They are committing the "mind-reading phenomenon" and are setting themselves up for frustration.

CASE   Karen, a supervisor in a bank, places a high priority on certain tasks but doesn't clearly explain this to her staff. When Dan, Karen's administrative assistant, completes tasks she thinks are trivial instead of the ones to which she gives a high priority, she becomes angry. Karen's attitude is, "Why should I have to tell him which tasks are important? He ought to know!" Thus, Dan has no way of knowing he has done something wrong until Karen blows up at him.

As a result, a lot of energy is wasted by both Karen and Dan. Karen often refers to Dan as stupid and inconsiderate and blames him for her anger.

Assertive supervisors will take the initiative and let their employees know what they want done, how they want it done, and *why* it is important. Passively hoping the employee will guess what is wanted leads to resentment and poor time management. In one agency, funding depended on client numbers as reflected in monthly reports. The staff chronically turned in reports late. The supervisor had never let them know why the monthly reports were necessary. The staff assumed that the reports were just more bureaucratic busy work.

CASE   Adam, a supervisor for a large manufacturing plant, doesn't tell his group that he wants their quarterly reports done a certain way and that no other way will do. He spends hours seething when they organize their reports in a way he considers totally inadequate. He has high standards, is a bit of a perfectionist, and can't understand why his workers just won't do things right!

An assertive supervisor would let his workers know specifically how he wanted the report done. Not telling his staff his expectations set Adam up to be angry and his workers to fail.

Another area that seems to cause problems is when supervisors do not let their employees know what they want when they delegate a task. To do a task well, the employee needs to know what has to be done, when it is to be done, and why it is to be done. Failure to take the time to give this information clearly is often the cause of lack of employee follow-through.

CASE   Jack was amazed during a seminar to recognize how general his instructions to his employees were. He didn't tell the employees when he wanted the work done, rarely explained specifics about how the task was to be done, and generally neglected to tell them why the task mattered. He assumed that they would know what he wanted when he said, "Give me a report on the Rino case." When Jack began to give assignments more clearly, he found himself more satisfied with his staff.

At the other extreme, some supervisors are very specific in demanding that employees do tasks in exactly the way they want them done. What they fail to do is listen to the other person's priorities. As a result, they are seen as arbitrary and dictatorial and may provoke surface compliance masking underground resistance. To overinstruct an employee can communicate a patronizing message: "You're too dumb to figure this out, so I'll have to tell you what to do."

EXERCISE 2.6

Three supervisors make a request of Tina. Which supervisor is most likely to be satisfied with the work he or she gets?

A. "Tina, write up a list of goals for our unit when you have some time."
B. "Tina, I want you to give me a list of what you think are the five most important goals of our unit for the next six months. I want them by Monday morning so that we can compile everyone's goals for our Tuesday staff meeting."
C. "Tina, I want you to stop what you're doing right now and write me up 15 goals for this department."

Answer: B. This supervisor makes a request that is specific about *what*, *when*, and *why* and that gives Tina some time to fit the request in with her priorities. This is likely to get the best results.

EXERCISE 2.7

1. Think of a time when someone was disappointed in your work. What did you need to know to do the job the way he or she wanted?

2. When was the last time you looked at someone else's work and said to yourself, "He or she should have known. . ."?

   What did that person need to know in order to do the task the way you wanted it done?

What could you have done or said to get what you wanted?

3. Observe yourself over the next several days and see if you are effective in asking for what you want. Write any observation here.

_____

Part of risk-taking is setting limits. As distasteful as it is, your job will sometimes entail interacting with people who are hostile, pushy, or demanding. When dealing with these kinds of people, assertive supervisors will let them know how their behavior is affecting them and suggest another way to handle the situation.

CASE   Harriet, a supervisor in a savings and loan association, has a manager who doesn't take her seriously. When she makes suggestions, he puts her down with biting remarks. Harriet needs to let her manager know how his remarks are affecting her self-esteem and explore with him more productive ways for the two of them to interact.

When you set limits, others know who you are and how you want to be treated. It is a way of gaining respect. When you don't set limits, you allow others to pick on you. It is difficult not to walk on someone who lies down in front of you!

CASE   Steve's boss, Marie, frequently criticized him in front of his staff. He decided he would risk letting Marie know how her behavior was affecting his image in the eyes of his staff. He stated that he was willing to hear her criticisms, but not in front of his staff. The two of them worked out a mutually agreeable plan to have Marie state her criticisms in the privacy of her office.

On the other side of the coin, there are people who are extremely sensitive, take offense easily, and become defensive. These people develop a negative reputation that leads others to avoid them for fear of overstepping one of their too numerous boundaries.

CASE Harry, a supervisor in a meat-packing plant, has so many boundaries that people who work with him often feel they are walking on egg-shells. If someone interrupts him, for example, he loudly announces that the person is being rude and should be able to see he is busy. Others avoid Harry, even when they need his help, because they never know when he will aggressively explode at them.

To be an effective supervisor it is important to be able to let people know when they are overstepping your limits without stepping on them in the process.

EXERCISE 2.8 Which of these supervisors do you think would be most respected by his or her co-workers?

A. Helen has an employee, Susan, who often becomes defensive and yells at her when Helen points out an error Susan made. Although Helen's discomfort at this is apparent to others, she hasn't said anything about it to Susan.
B. Stan feels slighted when employees disagree with anything he says, feeling that they are challenging his authority. He often says, "I can't get any respect around here!"
C. One of Monica's employees, Isaac, once began to scream at her in the general office. Monica quietly but firmly informed Isaac that she wasn't willing to be yelled at, although she was willing to discuss the problem in her office.

Answer: C. An assertive supervisor set limits without shutting the other person off or losing his or her cool.

KNOWING HOW TO SAY NO

The fourth building block to managing assertively is being able to say no. As a supervisor, your success relies heavily on your ability to meet goals, implement plans, distribute resources, and mediate and negotiate in your own unit. To carry out these functions effectively, you need to be able to establish boundaries and state what is OK and not OK with you. It is also important for you to know what you are willing and able to do with your limited time.

CASE   Bill feels that saying no will lead to his work unit disliking him. Consequently, he often says yes when he wants to say no. Because of this attitude, Bill feels that his office has no door on it and that he has no control over who comes in and out. He does not use his time effectively. Instead of establishing priorities based on the work to be done and the resources available, Bill goes along with the first request out of fear that the person will become angry if he says no. His reluctance to say no results in unmet deadlines, procrastination, and stress.

The ability to say no is crucial in two areas. The first is saying no to unwanted tasks imposed by peers and superiors. Without this ability you may be flooded with tasks that are not your responsibility, and you may not have time to do an effective job on tasks for which you are responsible.

CASE   Barbara is a supervisor responsible for a pool of six word processors in a large electronics company. Her staff serves ten supervisors who make high work demands. Kevin, a manager in an adjoining department, often asks Barbara to squeeze in a short report for him. His plea is, "You know that your people are much more accurate than the ones in my department, and it won't take very long." Unless Barbara learns to say no, her workers will be overwhelmed with unnecessary work.

The second area in which the ability to say no is crucial is the imposition of unrealistic deadlines. If you go along with an impossible deadline rather than negotiate a more realistic one, you will probably fail to complete the task on time, thus reducing your effectiveness in the eyes of your manager and your staff.

CASE   Erika, a supervisor in a large government agency, has a manager who waits until the last minute to give her a project to complete. If the actual time needed to get the project done is three days, the manager gives it to her one day before it is due. Until she is able to say no to this behavior, Erika will work overtime, feel resentment, and blame her manager for the stress the job causes her.

At the other extreme, supervisors can also get into difficulty if they say no so arbitrarily and dictatorially that others feel as if the supervisor lacks concern for them and their needs. There are times when you need to say yes to encourage and develop your employees, even when you might want to say no. Constant, hostile, or aggressive refusals can intimidate potentially involved and creative employees, causing them to leave or to do only the minimum on the job.

CASE   Jim, the head technician in a large metropolitan medical unit, is an expert at saying no. His staff knows whatever they ask, the answer will probably be no, often with an added put-down about "wasting time when you should have known better."

An assertive supervisor will say no when necessary to protect the distribution of time and resources so that the goals of the unit can be met. However, it is important to say no in a manner that shows respect for the other person and encourages continued participation.

EXERCISE 2.9

Which supervisor do you think is most likely to be effective in getting the job done?

A. Marcie sorts the work in her word processing unit according to priorities. She sometimes must disappoint a manager by letting him or her know that the work won't be ready by the time he or she requested.
B. When Teri's secretaries have a lot to do, she gets very angry at people who bring in more work. She has no hesitation about letting them know that the typists are just too busy.
C. Philip wants to please all of the managers to whom his typists report. He rarely says no to a request unless he's in a serious crisis.

Answer: A. A supervisor who sets priorities will know when the work will be completed, what can be done in a given time, and when he or she must say no to unreasonable requests. Initially, saying no may annoy people, but it will pay off when people trust you to deliver what and when you say you will.

EXERCISE 2.10

1. How do you think a workgroup's performance would be affected by a supervisor who often said no arbitrarily and without good reason?

2. How do you think a workgroup's performance would be affected by a supervisor who didn't say no when it was appropriate?

3. When is the last time you didn't say no and wished you **had?** What happened?

___

KNOWING HOW TO GIVE CONSTRUCTIVE FEEDBACK

The fifth building block to being an assertive supervisor is knowing how to give constructive feedback. One of the major barriers to being able to express negative feedback is the beliefs you may have about stating criticisms.

CASE   Ken, a supervisor for a small electronics company, was raised with the belief that "You shouldn't hurt anyone's feelings" and "If you can't say anything nice, don't say anything at all." As a result, he avoids providing correction to his staff even when their performance interferes with getting the work done properly. When he does correct someone, he does it in such a wishy-washy way that his correction has no impact.

Most supervisors have difficulty providing corrective feedback because they have difficulty receiving it themselves. People often respond to how the criticism is stated rather than to what is being said. Generally speaking, people want to improve at what they are doing, but when criticisms are stated with a fault-finding attitude and expressed with judgments and threats, it is understandable that the person receiving the criticism may respond with anger, hurt, or defensiveness.

CASE   Jack, a chemist in a large company, feels that his supervisor, Paul, criticizes him unjustly. Paul points out Jack's mistakes by telling him how incompetent he is and often threatens him by saying that if Jack fails to shape up, he'll wind up getting fired. Jack isn't really sure what he has done wrong; when he asks, the response is, "You should know." Jack leaves these confrontations feeling resentful and spends the rest of the day either fuming or feeling hurt. The result of the criticism is increased tension and a strong desire to avoid letting Paul find out about problems.

An assertive supervisor will call attention to a problem in a way that motivates the employee to correct it. This is done by letting the employee know what he or she needs to change, that is, stating what should be done about it.

Constructive Feedback

- Is stated in specific terms instead of vague, general ones

- Is directed at behavior, rather than personalities

- Is an observation of events, rather than labels or emotional judgment

- Focuses on a coaching style instead of put-downs

- Allows the receiver to solve his or her problems

EXERCISE 2.11

Which criticism would be most likely to lead the employee to correct his behavior?

A. "Ted, you never do anything right. If you paid attention, you wouldn't make such dumb mistakes. You should be able to do this; after all, you've worked here three months."

B. "Ted, I think you could be just a little more careful when you complete the time sheets."

C. "Ted, the time sheets for Johnson and Thomas weren't completed on time. When you don't complete them on time, it means Mary has to stay late to get the checks out on time. What can you do in the future so that the time sheets are completed on time?"

Answer: C. The corrective feedback is specific about what the problem is and why it is a problem, and it gives Ted the opportunity to solve the problem himself. It avoids name calling and personal put-downs and minimizes defensive behavior.

EXERCISE 2.12

1. Think of a time when someone corrected you effectively. What did that person do?

2. Think of a time when someone corrected you ineffectively. What did that person do?

3. Have you avoided correcting an employee recently? What's stopping you?

4. When you give corrective feedback to someone, what usually occurs?

5. Note one step you could take to improve the way you give corrective feedback.

HANDLING CRITICISM

The sixth building block to managing assertively is the ability to handle criticism from others without being defensive or upset. There are several factors that may lead you to handle criticism emotionally rather than effectively:

- Taking the criticism personally instead of seeing it as corrective feedback
- Failing to separate founded from unfounded criticism
- Reading into the criticism some message that isn't there
- Seeing the criticism as an invitation to get angry or to judge oneself harshly or punitively
- Failing to get specifics and examples of what is being criticized
- Believing that expressing criticism is bad or wrong.

CASE   Sandra, a social-work supervisor, has found that she can handle criticisms more effectively by learning to be aware of her feelings while being criticized. Sandra has discovered that there are several different kinds of criticisms. Some people try to "get her goat" by teasing her. Others criticize her when they are feeling frustrated, using her as a way to release their negative feelings and "blow off steam." Still others criticize her to provide her with information about problems that need to be solved.

Sandra has learned to recognize the type of criticism being directed at her and to then choose the appropriate response. She has found, for instance, that the teasing kind of criticism requires either limit-setting or a humorous response. She has the most difficulty with the "blowing off steam" kind of criticism. But if she doesn't take it personally and concentrates on understanding that it is an emotional release that doesn't involve her directly, she is able to stop herself from getting caught up emotionally.

When it is the problem-solving kind of criticism, she helps the person tell her what she has been doing incorrectly in specific terms, asking him or her for the reasons it is a problem and finding out what should be done about it. With this information, Sandra can effectively evaluate the problem and decide on a course of action agreeable both to her and to her critic.

EXERCISE 2.13

Suppose an employee said to a supervisor, "You're always picking on me. You never say anything bad about Joe." Which supervisor's response shows the most effective handling of the criticism?

A. "I'm really sorry. I don't mean to pick on you. I'll be more careful from now on."
B. "What specifically did I do that made you feel picked on? Let's talk about how this happens and look at ways to deal with it."
C. "What do you mean, I never say anything bad about Joe? If you were half as good a worker as Joe, I wouldn't have to pick on you!"

Answer: B. This response illustrates an effective way of handling one's feelings. "You pick on me" doesn't really tell the supervisor what the problem is. It is important to uncover what the employee means by that phrase. Apologizing or attacking cuts off further exploration of the problem, whereas asking for specifics and encouraging further discussion moves the interaction into problem solving.

EXERCISE 2.14

1. Think of a time you gave corrective feedback to someone and got good results. Describe what happened.

2. Now, think of a time you gave corrective feedback and got results you didn't like. Describe what happened.

3. How did the good-result incident differ from the bad-result incident?

KNOWING HOW TO EXPRESS AND
RECEIVE POSITIVE FEEDBACK

The seventh building block to managing assertively is the skill of giving and receiving positive feedback. Some supervisors have a difficult time doing this because of the beliefs they hold, such as "Why should I have to show my appreciation? They get pay checks just like me, don't they?" or "When you give people too much attention, they won't work hard" or "It's not my job to make people feel good; it's my job to get the work out." However, an effective supervisor knows that people are motivated when they are appreciated, treated with respect, and given credit for a job well done.

These same supervisors will often have difficulty receiving positive recognition because of other kinds of beliefs, "You shouldn't brag," "You shouldn't think well of yourself," "It's wrong to say nice things about yourself." They may have heard these expressions over and over again in childhood. Most children have had very little modeling of adults giving and accepting effective positive feedback. More than likely we would observe adults put down or deny compliments. As a result, many people have difficulty receiving positive feedback.

CASE Anna, a supervisor of a staff of six, works for an insurance broker. She can always be counted on to get the job done and is loyal and responsible. When Anna's broker pays her a compliment, she often responds with "Anyone could have done it," or "If it wasn't for my staff, I wouldn't have accomplished the task," or "I could have done it better." What Anna doesn't realize is that, when she denies or puts down the compliment, she is in essence discounting the positive evaluation of the giver—she is putting down the one giving the compliment. She could simply say "Thank you" or "I appreciate your noticing."

In addition to this early program, some supervisors get caught up in the "managing by exception" dilemma. This occurs when a supervisor pays attention only to what goes wrong and ignores what is done correctly or well.

CASE Sam has a supervisor, Todd, who believes that "if the employees do something right, that's to be expected; if they do it wrong, they should be corrected." Thus, Todd acknowledges only Sam's mistakes. Even when Sam goes out of his way on a project, Todd makes no comment.

Sam has begun to feel, "Why bother? No one notices anyway." He has begun to use his energy figuring out how to avoid getting jumped on instead of thinking about how to do the job well. Why should Sam risk doing anything creative and take the chance of being criticized?

The interesting thing about Sam and Todd's relationship is that Todd never sees Sam as a self-motivated employee. Because of his beliefs, Todd filters out of his awareness the things Sam does that are self-motivated and only sees the things that he doesn't like. Sam, in turn, blames Todd for his lack of motivation and enthusiasm for his job. Thus, each man blames the other for lousy feelings. A major barrier to problem solving is the failure of those having the problem to take responsibility for their contributions to the problem. One of the gravest mistakes people can make is to feel that they do not manage their own jobs.

On the other hand, many supervisors believe that positive reinforcement rather than punishment is a more effective way to change behavior. They know how good they feel when they are acknowledged and recognized for having accomplished something. Realizing how this affects them, they know that recognition will have a positive effect on those they supervise.

CASE Rosa, a supervisor of an accounting department, is the type of supervisor for whom the staff puts out that little extra bit of effort. She gives corrective feedback when appropriate, but she is also generous with her appreciation of a job well done. Her employees know that extra effort will be acknowledged both to them and to others. She can be overheard telling her superiors about the good work one of her staff members has done.

EXERCISE 2.15   Identify the supervisor who would be most likely to have the most highly motivated employees.

A. Harold makes a point of acknowledging good work or outstanding performance. He also points out difficulties when performance isn't meeting standards.
B. Jim feels that employees need a great deal of praise to feel good about themselves. As a consequence, he lavishes praise on almost all of the work he receives.
C. Phil believes that praise only causes dissension among people. He rarely says anything about work unless it is done wrong.

Answer: A. Harold acknowledges and supports good work and gives clear corrective feedback on work that doesn't meet standards, so that employees can tell the difference. Indiscriminant praise or complete lack of positive feedback both tend to support poor performance.

EXERCISE 2.16

1. Think of someone on the job with whom you are having difficulty. How do you respond to this individual in a negative way?

   How do you acknowledge this individual in a positive way?

2. What possible changes in the way you interact with a difficult person could lead to a more positive relationship with him or her?

KNOWING WHAT YOU WANT

The eighth building block to managing assertively is knowing what you want, setting goals, and developing a plan to accomplish them. Often it is tempting to sit back and wish that things were different. But people who waste their energies on "if only . . ." aren't doing what they need to do to be successful. Assertive supervision relies heavily on persistence, perseverance, and the unwillingness to give up despite obstacles. The following chronology in the life of a certain politician exemplifies this.

1832—Lost job

1832—Defeated in race for legislature

1833—Failed in private business

1834—Elected to legislature

1835—Sweetheart died

1836—Nervous breakdown

1836—Defeated for house speaker

1843—Defeated for nomination to Congress

1846—Elected to Congress

1848—Lost renomination to Congress

1849—Ran for land officer and lost

1854—Defeated for Senate

1856—Defeated for nomination for Vice-President of the United States

1858—Defeated for Senate again

1860—Elected President of the United States

The politician who suffered these ups and downs was Abraham Lincoln. President Lincoln's story exemplifies the importance of not letting obstacles cause a person to give up. He focused on the next project to accomplish.

Another major element of success is taking the time to diagnose the system in which you work (in terms of who has the power) the types of personalities with whom you must work, and the kind of organizational structure with which you must deal. Vivian is an example of a supervisor who overcame an obstacle by diagnosing the personality of her supervisor.

CASE   Vivian, a word-processing supervisor, needed new equipment for the three newest workers on her staff. She mentioned it to her manager, who said she would look into it. However, Vivian's manager had a "don't-rock-the-boat" personality and was unwilling to be active in any changes. Six months later, Vivian still hadn't gotten her new equipment.

Instead of passively saying, "if only . . .," Vivian began to do her homework.

She started to collect data on the differences in productivity between workers on the old equipment and those using new equipment. She recorded the number of days lost due to failure of the old equipment. She knew that she could send a memo covering these points to her manager and to the general manager of the department without causing problems, so she did. She also presented her request and her research verbally to her manager and the general manager. Within two months, she got the new equipment.

Part of the diagnosing process is examining the reality of the situation. Although the direct approach is usually best, in some situations it is not.

CASE Jay, a systems analyst supervisor, knew that his manager most often said no to plans that didn't come to him from above. Jay knew that approaching him directly about a new accounting program he had developed probably wouldn't work. Because Jay had done his homework, he knew that his plan would save his department $25,000 to $27,000 a year in time saved.

Jay worked out a plan to casually mention his ideas to the department head at the next committee meeting that both of them attended. When he did, the department head was most interested in the possible savings. Within one month, Jay's manager asked him to research other systems that could be used to save time over the current accounting program. Jay, thus, had the opportunity to present his idea.

The approach you should use depends on the person with whom you are dealing and what the situation is. Assertive supervisors learn to be flexible and versatile, knowing that success is based on adapting their style to others, rather than expecting others to adapt to them.

Finally, setting long-range personal and professional goals will take you a long way toward obtaining the position in the organization you want. This includes personal development as well as on-the-job skill building. Supervisors who know both their strengths and the areas in which they need improvement will be more successful in reaching the goals they set for themselves. Success requires you to plan effective strategies for bringing about positive change.

EXERCISE 2.17 A badly designed accounting form has been introduced from higher management. Identify which supervisor would be most likely to get the new accounting form changed.

A. Gary goes directly to his superior and announces that the new form simply doesn't work and that he and his staff won't use it.
B. Carol does some checking to see who developed the new form and why it was adopted. She surveys all the staff to get specific feedback about problems with the new form. Once she has the data, she arranges a meeting with her superior and the general manager to discuss possible changes.
C. Jerry complains a great deal to his staff and peers about the "stupid" new accounting form. He is convinced that the general manager will soon realize the new form is ineffective.

Answer: B. Carol does her homework, explores the power dynamics of the situation, and then presents her case to the people in authority. A is too aggressive; C is too passive.

EXERCISE 2.18

The importance of goals has been stressed in this section. Take a moment to think of the things you have learned in this chapter. Pick one thing that has the most significance for you. Develop a three-step plan of action to put it into practice.

1. Describe what you identified as the most significant point for you.

2. Describe the first step you will take to start putting this goal into practice.

3. Describe here the second step you will take.

4. Describe here the third step you will take.

5. Note here how you will know when you have accomplished this goal.

I have mentioned throughout this chapter that knowing yourself is important to be an assertive supervisor. You have probably become aware that some of the skills covered in this chapter are ones you already possess, whereas others are more difficult for you. You will find it useful to assess your behaviors and skills to identify those on which you need to work and those on which you don't. The following exercise will help.

| **ASSESSMENT** | **Managing Assertively—Self-Assessment** |

The following statements illustrate some behaviors with which supervisors have difficulty. Put an X on the continuum that most nearly describes how you see yourself in regard to each behavioral statement.

Example: I can refuse unreasonable requests by employees.

Always ____X_____ Never

You would put an X on the point of the continuum that comes closest to how easy or how difficult it is for you to do this behavior. In the above example, the X placed where it is on the continuum indicates that this person sees himself or herself being able to refuse unreasonable requests almost always and, thus, won't have too much trouble saying no. If he or she had difficulty with this behavior, the X would be closer to the end of the continuum marked "Never."

1. When I am disturbed about what someone is doing, I can say so.

   Always _____ Never

2. I take the initiative to cut short telephone calls when I am busy.

   Always _____ Never

3. When someone starts talking right in the middle of my conversation, I am able to express my feelings about the interruption.

   Always _____ Never

4. When a person continually teases me, I am able to express my displeasure.

   Always _____ Never

5. When someone I respect expresses opinions with which I strongly disagree, I state my own point of view.

   Always _____ Never

6. I am inclined to be overly apologetic.

   Always _____ Never

7. When a peer criticizes me unjustifiably, I am able to express my point of view.

Always _____ Never

8. When necessary, I am able to confront a domineering person.

Always _____ Never

9. If I hear that another is spreading false rumors about me, I can go directly to him or her to correct the situation.

Always _____ Never

10. I am able to give compliments and recognition to those I supervise.

Always _____ Never

11. I am able to give corrective feedback to those I supervise.

Always _____ Never

12. I am able to ask employees to do unpleasant tasks.

Always _____ Never

13. I am able to handle an angry person in a calm way.

Always _____ Never

14. I am able to handle criticism effectively.

Always _____ Never

15. I state my limits and expectations to those who work with me.

Always _____ Never

16. I generally express my negative feelings.

Always _____ Never

17. I avoid unpleasant situations for fear I won't be able to handle them effectively.

Always _____ Never

18. I remain calm and rational in stressful situations.

Always _____ Never

19. I am able to turn in a poor evaluation of one of my employees without agonizing over it.

Always _____ Never

20. I feel comfortable when called on to take sides in employee disputes.

Always _____ Never

Discussion of Assessment

Take a moment to review your assessment. Look for things you learned about yourself.

1. Make a notation below of the behaviors with which you are pleased and want to continue doing.

How do these behaviors affect you as a supervisor?

2. Make a notation below of the behaviors you think need improvement.

How do these behaviors affect you as a supervisor?

3. Make an action statement for change. For example, "I will replace the unassertive behavior that is interfering with my being an assertive supervisor. At the end of each day, I will analyze how I behaved in this new way and reward myself for reaching my goal."

Your action statement for change:

SUMMARY

In this chapter, you learned the eight building blocks to managing assertively: building self-esteem, knowing how to listen, taking risks, knowing how to say no, knowing how to express criticism in a constructive manner, handling criticism, knowing how to express and receive positive feedback, and knowing what you want. You completed several exercises that assisted you in understanding and applying the concepts related to the building blocks. In order to know yourself better, you completed a self-awareness assessment that gave you a profile on the kinds of assertive supervisory behaviors you were already doing well and others on which you need to work.

3 Supervisory Styles: Assertive–Aggressive–Passive

I don't believe in circumstances. The people who get on in this world are the people who look for the circumstances they want, and if they don't find them, make them.

George Bernard Shaw

Managing assertively involves developing trust and confidence in those you supervise. No one approach could be best for handling all those you supervise. However, managing assertively provides a framework that can assist you in developing a better understanding of how to handle people-related problems.

As stated in Chapter 1, you accomplish very little alone. For you to have a productive work group, you need to develop a team in which common objectives are held and the group members are interacting with each other in an assertive manner. This means that disorganized efforts of individuals are minimized so that your work group is working toward the attainment of group goals. The specific supervisory methods used will depend on various factors at play in the work environment at a particular time.

EXERCISE 3.1   **Distinguishing Between Styles of Supervision**

To distinguish between the three styles, you will examine each type of response in specific situations. After reading the following situations, classify each response according to whether you think it is *assertive, aggressive,* or *passive*.

1. Don, a supervisor in a bank, has been doing his job exceptionally well and expects a salary increase. When he discusses it with his manager, his manager says that the company cannot afford it now and that Don must wait six months. Don responds:

    A. "Fine, I'll check with you then." _____
    B. "I believe the increase I'm requesting is reasonable, and you agree that my responsibilities have increased. I'd like to discuss it further." _____
    C. "I was promised this raise. I deserve it, and I want it now!" _____

2. Kathy is the only female supervisor at a meeting with a group of male colleagues, and she is asked to act as the secretary. She responds:

    A. "Sure, I'd be happy to." _____
    B. "I'd like to let someone else take his turn today. If you'll recall, I took the minutes at the last meeting." _____
    C. "I resent that request. Just because I'm a woman doesn't mean that I'm a secretary." _____

3. Harold is coordinating a project with a supervisor from another department, but he finds that he is doing all the work. Harold says:

    A. "You're not doing your part. If I don't get some cooperation, I'm going to tell the boss." _____
    B. "On paper, we are coordinating this project, yet I see that I'm doing all the work. I'd like to talk with you about changing this." _____
    C. Nothing. Harold continues to do all the work by himself by staying late. _____

4. Daniel is a supervisor of the purchasing unit. A manager from another department requests extra materials from him. Daniel has had trouble meeting his budget goals and prefers not to make these extra materials available. Daniel says:

    A. "I just can't provide these extra materials right now. I might be able to get them to you next week. Is that okay?" _____
    B. "You shouldn't be asking me for extra materials. I'm over budget myself, so I won't be able to send them to you." _____
    C. "Presently I'm having difficulty meeting my budget, and I prefer not making extra materials available unless it's essential. Tell me more about your problem, and let's explore some of the ways we might approach it." _____

5. Peggy has an employee who is not performing in accordance with goals that she and the employee have discussed on several occasions. When reviewing the employee's performance, Peggy says:

A. "It looks to me as if you are just careless and irresponsible, or maybe you just don't have what it takes to do this job." _____

B. "You know it is my job to bring you in every once in a while and talk over how things are going. I hope this doesn't upset you, and I want to be as fair and helpful as I can. I don't see any reason why we can't have a friendly talk and review how things have been going." _____

C. "We have talked several times about your work goals. The results are not up to the level we agreed upon. It is not acceptable that the goals we set are not accomplished. I want to discuss with you the consequences of your continuing to perform in this manner." _____

Answers:

1B, 2B, 3B, 4C, and 5C are *assertive* responses.

1C, 2C, 3A, 4B, and 5A are *aggressive* responses.

1A, 2A, 3C, 4A, and 5B are *passive* responses.

You have seen some examples of each of the three supervisory styles. This and the following sections discuss the characteristic behaviors of each.

CASE Peter is, without a doubt, the best-liked supervisor in the company. His door is always open, and his employees pass through it frequently seeking extra time off for this reason and that. No other supervisor is more lavish with praise at performance-evaluation time.

But all is not well. Production in Peter's unit is steadily slipping. Peter is so fearful of being disliked that he doesn't state his expectations clearly and accedes to unreasonable requests. He has several mottos that interfere with his effectiveness: "I shouldn't rock the boat," "I don't want to make waves." These beliefs lead to a passive style that results in loss of respect from his staff. And since Peter doesn't take a stand with management on issues that are important to his work group, his top performers leave to take positions where they have greater visibility and possibility for advancement.

Most often, passive behavior results in feelings of fear, anxiety, guilt, and physical and emotional stress. Passive supervisors tend to feel that outside forces are controlling them; they have low self-esteem and a negative self-image. Excessively passive behavior leads to a noncooperative work group that controls what is done in the unit. It is important to know that there are other factors that could make a passive response the best one. A responsible and hard-working *staff,* for example, would allow you to sit back and let them do the work. If you always directed their performance, they could perceive you as oversupervising and could think you don't trust them.

Timing can determine whether it is appropriate to be assertive or passive. Suppose you have an important matter to work out with your manager; but it is 4:30 p.m., quitting time is 5 p.m., the manager has had a hectic day, and you will need at least 20 minutes to discuss the problem. Considering these factors, you'd probably be better off talking to him the next day when he has time and doesn't feel stressed.

The *intensity of your feelings* may be significant. When someone feels strongly about a situation, he or she often doesn't think too rationally about it. Sometimes you would be better off leaving the matter alone until the next day. Otherwise, you might say things you don't really mean when expressing them from a strong emotional level.

The *emotional level of the other person* may play a role. Sometimes the other person is so emotionally charged that your best choice is to passively listen and to then determine another time when the situation can be dealt with more calmly.

As you become aware of the differences among the three supervisory styles, you will probably notice other times when the passive style would be most appropriate.

EXERCISE 3.2

Take a moment to reflect on an occasion when you did not respond in a passive way but later decided that passive would have been better. Note your thoughts here:

ELEMENTS OF THE PASSIVE STYLE

As a way to identify the overall behavioral patterns of the three styles, I have broken each style into nine categories: nonverbal cues, behavior, verbal cues, mottos and beliefs, characteristics, confrontation and problem solving, feelings felt, communication style, and the effect on self and others. The purpose of this is to assist you in thoroughly examining each style so that you will have a better understanding of what that style is like in a variety of ways.

As you read over these behaviors, make a mental note of those that describe you.

Nonverbal Cues

Gestures:	• Wrings hands
	• Fidgets with pen, pencil, or other items or parts of the body or clothing
	• Talks with hand over mouth
	• Other nervous gestures
	• Nods head often to come across as agreeable
Facial expression:	• Lack of expression
	• Bored look
	• Anxious
	• Pouting, sulking look
	• Blank look
	• Smiles and nods in agreement
Eye contact:	• Seldom looks at others
	• Downcast eyes, looks down to the ground
	• Roving eyes, looks all around
Posture:	• Slumped
	• Crooked
	• Uneven
Tone of voice:	• Weak
	• Low or meek
	• Timid, whiny
	• Questioning
Rate of speech:	• Fast—when feeling anxious
	• Hesitant—when feeling doubtful

Behavior

• Goes off in huff to manipulate
• Sighs a lot

- Hides feelings, keeps them inside
- Says he or she is angry, yet smiles
- Tries to sit on both sides of the fence to avoid conflict
- Afraid to take risks
- Stage fright when speaking in front of a group
- Clams up when he or she feels treated unfairly
- Asks permission when it isn't necessary
- Complains instead of taking action
- Buys the approval of others so that he or she is often seen as selfless, a good sport, easygoing
- Gets others to stand up for him or her
- Kowtows to the desires and commands of others
- Falls into "poor little me" trap
- Blames others for failings

Verbal Cues

- "Yes . . . sure . . . okay . . . right . . ."
- "I wish . . ."
- "If only . . ."
- "I can't . . ."
- "I never (always) . . ."
- "I'll try . . ."
- "I ought to . . ."
- "I should (have got to) . . ."
- "I'd better . . ."
- "I'm sorry, but . . ."
- "You may not believe this, but . . ."
- "This may seem silly, but . . ."
- "I'll be honest with you . . ."
- "This is probably wrong, but . . ."
- "I hate to tell you this . . ."
- "May I ask you a question?"

Mottos and Beliefs

- "Don't express your true feelings."
- "You shouldn't speak up until spoken to."
- "You must be nice."
- "Keep your opinions to yourself."
- "Don't make waves; if you do, you won't be liked."
- "Be agreeable at all times."

- "Don't disagree."
- "I am inadequate—not valuable."
- "Others have rights, I don't have any."

Characteristics

- Apologetic, self-conscious
- Self-doubting, submissive
- Unresponsive
- Trusts others, but not self
- Has difficulty accepting positive feedback
- Doesn't express own wants and feelings
- Inconspicuous, compliant
- Nice, helpful, easygoing
- When asked "Where do you want me to put this information?" often responds "Any place," "Anywhere," "I don't care"—then complains about what happened or blames others
- Misunderstood because his or her fears cause them to be indirect
- Allows others to make decisions for him or her, thus not getting what he or she wants
- Rarely achieves his or her goals
- Loses respect and power

Confrontation and Problem Solving

- Generally nonconfrontative
- Expends energy to avoid conflicts that are anxiety provoking because he or she feels powerless to do anything about them
- The more he or she tries to avoid anxiety-provoking situations and people, the greater the anxiety about facing them
- When faced with threatening and anxiety-provoking situations, feels he or she has no control over anxiety and, thus, is immobilized and controlled by it
- Gets cold feet when approaching someone about a difficult matter
- Gets others to do his or her choosing because he or she doesn't want to be responsible for what happens

- Plays dumb and confused and, thus, becomes a burden
- Hesitates to speak up
- Avoids, leaves, ignores, postpones
- Lets others decide
- Withdraws, is sullen and silent
- Doubts his or her ability to make decisions or solve problems
- Noncommittal
- Abstains, doesn't argue
- Agrees externally while disagreeing internally

Feelings Felt

- Like a doormat
- Victimized, defeated
- Resentful, powerless
- Controlled, manipulated
- Inferior
- Depressed
- Embarrassed
- Anxious
- Fearful

Communication Style

- Is indirect
- Agrees to almost everything
- Doesn't speak up
- Hesitates
- Doesn't interrupt to get wants met

Effects

On self:
- Gives up being him or herself
- Physical problems, headache, back pains

On others:
- Feels disgust toward passive person
- Takes care of them and protects them
- Builds dependency relationships
- Gets blamed for making wrong decisions
- Tends to feel guilty about getting own way so often
- Doesn't know where he or she stands

As you read this information, you probably became more aware of how a passive style of supervision can result in numerous people problems. A supervisor weakens his or her position by negating self in front of others and by being overly apologetic. People generally respect someone who is self-confident and open to his or her strengths and abilities while admitting to the weaker areas of self; on the other hand, they disrespect downgrading behavior.

It is difficult to be assertive when a person is "catastrophizing" in his head by thinking, "If I ask them to do this unpleasant task, they won't like me" or "If I stand up to them on this difficult issue, they'll quit." People who catastrophize expect horrible consequences, even though such consequences will only happen once in a thousand times. Catastrophizing leads to feelings of fear and anxiety, which in turn lead to mistakes and poor performance.

PASSIVE AGGRESSIVE/HIDDEN AGGRESSIVE BEHAVIOR

Another important consequence of passive behavior needs to be examined. Excessively passive behavior can result in *passive aggressive behavior,* sometimes referred to as *hidden aggression.* The three styles can be viewed in terms of a continuum.

A major advantage of being assertive is that it gives you more flexibility and versatility on the continuum. A critical component of assertive behavior is operating from choice. It's like the difference between an eagle and a toad who are in need of an oasis of food and water. Because the eagle has a broad, expansive view, it sees the oasis just ahead, whereas the toad, who can only see its immediate area, cannot. This higher awareness allows the eagle to get the food and water it needs. However, the toad's narrow view of the world significantly reduces the possibility of it finding the oasis.

Because of this flexibility and higher awareness, assertive supervisors will have broader movement on the continuum. In some situations and with some people, they will be passive, as in the examples discussed earlier (page 46) of when passive can be positive. Those were examples of when you would move toward passive—of when you would be passive assertive.

The same is true for moving toward the aggressive end of the continuum. There will be times when you'll want to choose positive aggressive behavior. Such times could be when emergencies occur, when someone is violating the safety and security of others, or when a person is violating company etiquette and/or policies.

You may be asking yourself, what does all of this have to do with passive aggressive behavior? When you look at the continuum, it looks like the passive and aggressive behaviors are remote from each other. And, they generally are. However, when a person is behaving passive aggressively, both behaviors are being activated simultaneously. In other words, he or she is being aggressive in a passive manner. Because the two behaviors are at the extreme ends of the continuum, it appears they are opposites. But if the continuum is drawn this way:

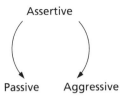

the two behaviors are very close to each other. What does this mean in terms of supervisory style?

CASE Virginia has a manager who usually manages her in an aggressive style. He puts her down in front of her staff, is demanding in his requests, is punitive when she makes mistakes, and is always "right," even when Virginia's suggestion would have worked better.

Virginia believes that she "must be nice, especially to people in authority" and feels that she is inadequate and unimportant; so, as a result, she says nothing. Instead of asserting herself and exploring ways the two of them could work better together, she responds to his aggressive style by avoiding conflict and confrontation—moving into the passive-aggressive style.

Thus, she is late getting her reports in, forgets to follow through on matters that are important to her manager, and is sick on days when he really needs her. She doesn't do these things to excess, but just enough to frustrate him and make his life a little miserable.

CASE Stephen is a member of a self-directing team. He feels that, because of his years on the job, he is more qualified than the others to solve problems that come before the group. He doesn't listen to the other team mem-

bers; instead, he does most of the talking. When he does allow anyone to talk, he is quick to interrupt and tell the person how wrong his or her idea is.

The group is hesitant to confront him assertively because they are afraid of what he'll do. As a result, they don't give Stephen information he needs to get his portion of the task done on time, meetings often start late, and the morale of the group is low.

People usually don't move into this passive aggressive mode deliberately; it's not a conscious decision but one made compulsively and automatically because of conditioning. It is a defense mechanism for survival in an environment where the person feels powerless. In other words, it is a way to defy, strike back, and resist being treated like a nonperson, a "thing."

ANALYZING THE AGGRESSIVE STYLE

In this society, the word *aggressive* has taken on a very negative meaning because aggressive people often express their feelings at the expense of others. They have the attitude that "I have rights, others don't; what you want is less important than what I want."

CASE   John is the one supervisor for whom nobody wants to work. He's a "no-nonsense guy" who prides himself on "really whipping his workers into shape." He gets the job done—but he leaves a wake of hard feelings, bitterness, and requests for transfers.

He overpowers his staff by his know-it-all attitude and his belief that he is never wrong. During a staff meeting, he dominates the discussion and then gets angry because no one will speak up. His staff copes with his aggressive style by resisting, forming alliances, and covering up. Although he has control over how things are done, he has to pay for it in terms of time and energy spent supervising his staff—a kind of self-imposed servitude.

Excessive use of the aggressive style often perpetuates in others the passive-aggressive mode discussed earlier. Aggressive people create a double bind for themselves: they do not respect anyone they can dominate, yet they fear an equal relationship. In addition, this style dehumanizes the aggressor as much as it does those being attacked.

Everyone has an inborn need to love people and to use things. The aggressive supervisor has turned this around: He or she uses people and loves things. When someone uses another person, the one being used feels like a nonperson, and his or her self-esteem is depleted. When one depletes another's self-esteem, one diminishes oneself.

The aggressive style can be positive when you are in the OK–OK attitude. There will be times when you need to take charge aggressively. From my experience, being positive aggressive makes it more difficult to have the other person perceive you as positive because, when most people behave aggressively, they are usually coming from the OK–Not OK attitude. Because of this, the other person can misjudge your behavior. The critical component is your OK attitude.

In some situations, the aggressive style would be the best response. If someone *goes against company rules,* aggression may be in order. Suppose a staff member defies the rules even after you have pointed it out and stated your limits. The first time around, you don't want to use a club when a light tap will do. However, if this is the third or fourth time, you will want to react in proportion to the deed. In other words, you'll want to use more "muscle" and make the consequences of the behavior explicit.

Another situation would be dealing with an *angry, hostile,* or *demanding* person. When handling this type of person, you would do well to move toward the aggressive side of the assertive mode. You would want to let the person know how the behavior is affecting you and suggest another way to deal with what is going on.

You would want to take charge and be aggressive in an emergency situation. This would not be a time to call a meeting to get a consensus of the correct action. Another time to take action and deal directly with the person is if someone is violating the safety or security of others.

Generally speaking, move to the aggressive side of the assertive mode when handling difficult people. Approach them firmly and with clear intentions. (These kinds of people will be dealt with more thoroughly in Chapter 6.)

EXERCISE 3.3

Take a moment to reflect on an occasion when you did not respond in an aggressive way but later decided that assertive would have been better. Note your thoughts here:

ELEMENTS OF THE AGGRESSIVE STYLE

The following are the overall behavioral patterns of the aggressive style. As you read over this style, make a mental note of the behaviors with which you have the most difficulty handling in others.

Nonverbal Cues

Gestures:
- Points, shakes finger
- Pushes
- Pounds table
- Slams doors
- Throws things

Facial expression:
- Frowns
- Rolls eyes when disgusted
- Squints eyes critically

Eye contact:
- Glares
- Stares
- Holds contact

Posture:
- Rigid
- Hands on hips
- Fists clenched

Tone of voice:
- Critical

Rate of speech:	• Loud, yelling, and rasping
	• Shrill
	• Gruff
	• Fast, quick
	• Precise

Behavior

- Puts others down
- May respond too vigorously, making a negative impression, and later be sorry for it
- Often wants to be first, is competitive
- Walks fast and ahead of others
- Doesn't ever think they are wrong
- Takes over a group
- Is bossy, pushy
- Takes charge, task-oriented, accomplishes things
- Moves into people's space, overpowers
- Jumps on others, pushes people around
- Has know-it-all attitude
- Demands center stage
- Won't see other's point of view
- Is emotional and expressive
- Uses others as things ("thinging people")
- Doesn't show appreciation
- Won't delegate responsibility

Verbal Cues

- "You must (should, ought, better)"
- "You always (never)"
- Obscenities
- Abusive language
- "Why don't you . . ."
- "You know better than that."
- "You dummy, that's a stupid thing to do . . ."
- "Everyone knows that."
- "Don't do as I do, but as I say."
- "Don't ask why, just do it."

Mottos and Beliefs

- "I've got rights but you don't."

- "My feelings are more important than yours."
- "Everyone should be like me."
- "I am never wrong."
- "People should do what I ask without questioning me."
- "People ought to behave the way I think they should."

Characteristics

- Action oriented, often at the expense of others
- Direct to a fault
- Demanding, arrogant
- Domineering, bullying
- Opinionated
- Forceful, arbitrary
- Patronizing
- Belittling
- Authoritarian
- Self-righteous
- Punitive, critical
- Self-assured
- Self-initiative

Confrontation and Problem Solving

- Resolves conflicts while stepping on toes
- Must win arguments, threatens, attacks
- Has difficulty accepting defeat
- Confronts
- Initiates
- Operates from win/lose

Communication Style

- Berates others
- Is close minded
- Is direct
- Labels behavior
- Listens poorly
- Has difficulty seeing the other person's point of view

- Interrupts
- Talks fast
- Cuts people off in conversation
- Forces views on others
- Monopolizes discussions
- Gives nonconstructive criticism
- Calls people names

Feelings Felt

- Anger
- Resentment
- Hostility
- Frustration
- Irritation
- Annoyance
- Impatience

Effects

On self:

- Provokes counteraggression, alienation from others, ill health
- Makes enemies
- Creates own opposition
- Fosters own opposition
- Takes time and energy to oversupervise others
- Feels guilt for overbearing behavior
- Pays high price in human relationships
- Fosters resistance, defiance, sabotaging, striking back, forming alliances, lying, covering up
- Undermines respect

On others:

- Fosters fear
- Fosters compliance with resentment

As you noted the behaviors with which you have difficulty dealing, you probably thought to yourself, "I sure hope I'm not this way!" You will also notice that six of the nine common complaints of workers about their bosses listed at the beginning of Chapter 1 fit the aggressive supervisory style. In addition, when you wrote down the behaviors and characteristics of the worst boss you ever had, how many things did you note that fit the aggressive style?

ANALYZING THE ASSERTIVE STYLE

The assertive style is based on the Seven **Keys of Goodness** covered in the definition of managing assertively:

1. Influencing others in a positive way that encourages people to realize their potential

2. Practicing an active and initiating (rather than reacting) mode of behavior

3. Taking a caring position, emphasizing the positive nature of self and others

4. Exhibiting self-expression through which one stands up for his or her basic rights without denying the rights of others and without experiencing undue anxiety or guilt

5. Possessing a nonjudgmental attitude that diminishes the use of labels, stereotypes, and prejudices

6. Taking responsibility for oneself by not making other people responsible for who we are, what we do, and how we think and feel

7. Communicating wants, dislikes, and feelings in a clear, direct manner without threatening and attacking

These seven keys stress that each person has a unique, personal space that makes it a necessity that one be respected by those with whom he or she interacts. As a person moves outside his or her space into the common area where others are, it is that person's responsibility to respect the rights of others.

Responsibility is an important element of the assertive style—responsibility for oneself, not others! However, you are responsible for how you behave. Remember the Seven Keys of Goodness and the foundation of being assertive!

Part of the responsibility is setting limits to take care of yourself, while accepting the consequences of your actions. This means you state what you want without violating the rights of others.

CASE   Marilyn supervises a staff of ten people in the customer service department of a large computer company. Her group has the reputation of "making things happen." They seem able to do the impossible when an especially complex order has to be filled quickly. Morale is high in Marilyn's unit; team effort is obvious, and no one wants to transfer out.

Marilyn believes in recognizing a job well done and in providing corrective feedback when necessary, although the proportion of positive to corrective feedback is 80:20, since she emphasizes the positive. She believes it is important for her staff to know her limits and expectations and for her to know theirs. Marilyn clears up misunderstandings quickly so that negative feelings don't interfere with productivity and high performance.

She has promoted open communication among her staff so that they will express their true feelings openly and honestly, which has helped them to develop a mutual support system. Because she feels so strongly that the passive and aggressive styles distract from the professionalism of her work group, she has cultivated assertiveness in her staff. She has the following list of "My Assertive Human Rights" framed and hung in her office where everyone can see them.

My Assertive Human Rights

1. I have the right to take responsibility for the initiation of my behavior, thoughts, and emotions and to handle the consequences they may perpetuate.

2. I have the right to state my limits, expectations, and feelings about other people's behavior in a manner that respects their self-esteem.

3. I have the right to decide if I am responsible for solving other people's problems and to facilitate their solving their own problems.

4. I have the right to change my mind.

5. I have the right to make mistakes, to be responsible for them, and to learn from them.

6. I have the right to say, "I don't know."

7. I have the right to be treated with respect and to respect others.

8. I have the right to explain my position in the manner I think is most appropriate and to listen nonjudgmentally to the position of others.

9. I have the right to say "No," without feeling guilty.

10. I have the right to ask for clarification when I don't understand.

11. I have the right to ask for what I want, knowing that the other person has the right to refuse.

Marilyn's "My Assertive Human Rights" state in a nutshell the basic premises of managing assertively. You might want to study them carefully and reflect on how recognizing these rights would influence your way of supervising others. Remember, for every right there is a responsibility.

COMPONENTS OF THE ASSERTIVE STYLE

The assertive style includes four components:

- *Verbal*—Your spoken words
- *Cognitive*—Your mental processes
- *Emotional*—The level of your feelings and vocal tone and volume
- *Nonverbal*—Your body language, facial expressions, and eye contact

Your use of these components will strongly influence how your messages will be heard and will be accepted by the other person.

**Verbal
Component**

First, it is best to use words that indicate that you feel good about yourself as well as about other people. The words you use are critical because words represent who you are, what you believe, and how you think and feel. Your words carry energy—"In the beginning was the word . . ." Words help you connect with others or to distance yourself from them. You probably have noticed that words include a certain tone, a particular look, and a specific posture.

It is imperative that you listen to the words you use. This can be done by listening to how you talk about others. Are you describing their behavior nonjudgmentally rather than labeling or name calling? It's critical to refrain from using such phrases as "You should," "You ought to," "You've got to," "You always," "You never," and "You did this wrong." Avoid "red flag" words—words to which people are sensitive and to which they respond emotionally. Avoid being overly apologetic—stop using phrases like "I'll try," "I can't," or "I wish."

An assertive supervisor might replace should, ought to, have to, must, and so on, with such wording as:

- This is the way I want it done *or* like it done.
- This is the way we do it.
- These are the guidelines we follow.
- This is the procedure we use *or* system we follow.
- These are the laws (regulations) that we follow.

In place of "you never" or "you always," an assertive supervisor would be specific, such as:

- This happened three times last week.

- This is the second time you were late getting your paperwork to me.

- This was completed incorrectly.

- Let's review the steps you took.

The focus would be to approach the situation from a coaching assertive style rather than from a critical aggressive style.

If someone makes a request, the assertive supervisor would say "I'll do it" and give a time frame; or "I won't be able to do it" and suggest an alternative time, instead of just saying "I'll try." (Remember, trying is an activity not an accomplishment.) Instead of "I can't," they would say "I don't have enough information *or* resources *or* training to do what you ask. "I wish" is replaced with "I've decided," and a plan to get it done would be developed. (People who wish for things without a decision and plan usually don't get what they wish for.)

The following examples illustrate the points in regard to a supervisor calling attention to an employee's mistake.

Nonassertive Approach

1. "You did this wrong, again! You know you shouldn't do it this way!"

2. "I wish you would try not to make so many mistakes."

Assertive Approach

1. This particular procedure was done incorrectly. Let's review the steps you took and find out what happened.

2. Let's examine what is happening that is causing you to complete this task incorrectly. It's important to me that tasks are done without error.

Cognitive Component

The cognitive component entails what you go through internally, including all the things that interfere with your behaving in the manner you would like. People sometimes set such rigid requirements for themselves that it is almost impossible for them to be assertive. Others use negative self-labeling to talk themselves out of being assertive, thinking, "No one will listen to me, anyway" or "Why bother? I don't have anything of value to say." People often expect the worst to happen and then visualize it happening, followed by a negative affirmation such as, "I can't speak up, I'm so shy" or "I'll probably goof, so why try?" Most often, this is the result of a negative self-concept, which develops into self-defeating behavior.

Instead, it would be more useful to do just the opposite—expect to be successful at asserting yourself, then visualize it happening, followed by a positive affirmation such as, "I can speak up if I am prepared and have a plan" or "By stating my limits and expectations, I will have better working relationships." These positive and negative processes are illustrated by the charts in Figure 3.1.

Emotional Component

The emotional component includes the level of feelings expressed, the voice volume, and the tone of voice. It is important to state your message at an emotional level that fits the situation because your tone of voice plays a crucial role in how your message is received by the other person. Do you know someone who has a tone of voice that is grating to your

FIGURE 3.1

Positive and negative processes.

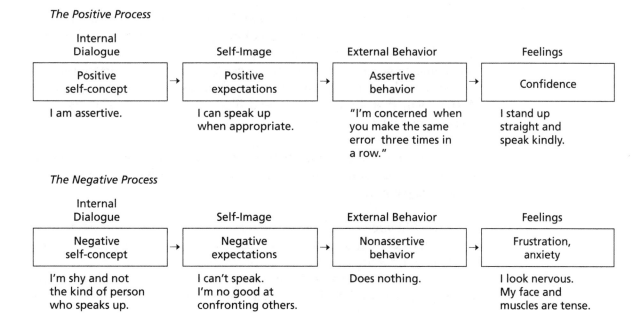

The Positive Process

Internal Dialogue	Self-Image	External Behavior	Feelings
Positive self-concept	Positive expectations	Assertive behavior	Confidence
I am assertive.	I can speak up when appropriate.	"I'm concerned when you make the same error three times in a row."	I stand up straight and speak kindly.

The Negative Process

Internal Dialogue	Self-Image	External Behavior	Feelings
Negative self-concept	Negative expectations	Nonassertive behavior	Frustration, anxiety
I'm shy and not the kind of person who speaks up.	I can't speak. I'm no good at confronting others.	Does nothing.	I look nervous. My face and muscles are tense.

ears—someone you would like to shut up as soon as he or she starts talking? Many people respond defensively to those who sound like their parents talking to them, perhaps because their voice tone has a condescending quality.

Nonverbal Component

The nonverbal component is extremely important. Much of what you say is expressed nonverbally. Research shows that nonverbal messages have the greatest impact on those with whom you communicate. The following is a breakdown of the various nonverbal behaviors:

• *Eye contact:* You can weaken an assertion by looking away when saying something assertive. It is best to keep eye contact throughout the message. Look directly at the other person to show that you are sincere and that the message is directed at her or him.

• *Facial expression:* Make your facial expression consistent with the mood and message. A confusing double message can be expressed when your facial expression does not agree with the message, e.g., smiling while expressing anger.

• *Silence:* You can use silence effectively by pausing to think or collect your thoughts.

• *Voice tone, inflection, or volume:* These can reduce or induce power. Whispering is seen as an indication of being scared or timid, whereas an overly loud voice is seen as aggressive. A level, well-modulated voice tone is convincing without being intimidating. Volume needs to match the importance of the situation, and the message needs to be stated definitively. A statement that goes up at the end like a question comes across as a passive statement.

• *Gestures:* Accent your message with appropriate gestures. Finger shaking or hand in fist can be seen as aggressive; wringing of hands can be seen as passive.

• *Body Language:* Assertive posture is relaxed rather than rigid, open rather than closed, straight rather than crooked. The weight of your message will be increased if you face the person, stand or sit appropriately close, and lean toward the person while holding your head erect. Have your arms relaxed and open, rather than folded tightly across your chest.

• *Rate of speech:* A normal and moderate rate of speech will have the best affect. If you state your message too quickly or too slowly, the listener could read this as hesitation, anxiety, or nervousness.

• *Timing:* Spontaneous expression will generally be your goal, since hesitation may diminish the effect of assertion. Select an appropriate occasion; speak to the boss in the office, not in front of others.

ELEMENTS OF THE ASSERTIVE STYLE

The following is the overall behavioral pattern of the assertive style. As you read over the behaviors, make a mental note of those behaviors you think would assist you in being more effective when managing others.

Nonverbal Cues

Gestures:	• Reaching out
	• Open
Facial expression:	• Attentive
	• Interested
	• Responsive
	• Consistent with what is being expressed
Eye contact:	• Direct
	• Friendly
Posture:	• Relaxed
	• Open
	• Level
Tone of voice:	• Medium
	• Volume appropriate
Rate of speech:	• Moderate
	• Consistent with situation

Behavior

• Tries alternate assertions when necessary
• Operates from choice
• Knows what is needed and develops a plan to get it
• Observes behavior rather than labeling it
• Accepts and respects self and others
• Is realistic in expectations

- Emphasizes the positive nature of self and others
- Takes responsibility
- Takes appropriate action toward getting what is wanted without denying rights of others

Verbal Cues

- "I choose to . . ."
- "What are the options?"
- "Who, where, when, how"
- "Let's talk it over."
- "What are the alternatives?"
- "I agree that I could have taken another course of action."

Mottos and Beliefs

- "It's OK to learn from mistakes."
- "Mistakes aren't final but are to be corrected."
- "I believe that myself and others are valuable."
- "I know that assertiveness doesn't mean that I always win, but that I handled the situation as effectively as possible."
- "I respect myself and others."
- "I give positive reinforcement to myself and others."
- "I have rights and so do others."
- "Operating from a nonjudgmental mode increases my effectiveness."

Characteristics

- Nonjudgmental
- Forgiving, understanding
- Action-oriented
- Firm
- Trusting
- Self-responsible
- Loving
- Compassionate
- Enthusiastic
- Confident

- Self-aware
- Positive self-concept and self-esteem
- Fair, just
- Consistent
- Tolerant, patient
- Open, flexible, versatile
- Persistent
- Playful
- Decisive

*Confrontation and
Problem Solving*

- Operate from win/win position
- Negotiates, bargains, trades off, compromises
- Solves problems by exploring alternatives
- Confronts problems at the time they happen
- Doesn't let negative feelings build up
- Initiates clearing up resentment and misunderstanding
- Learns problem-solving skills and applies them

Feelings Felt

- Joy
- Enthusiasm
- Excitement
- Well-being
- Even-temperedness

Communication Style

- Listens actively and effectively
- Has positive self-image
- States limits, expectations
- Says no to unreasonable requests
- Listens with understanding, nonjudgmentally
- States observations, not labels or judgments
- Is consistent in verbal and nonverbal communication
- Encourages feedback
- Is straightforward and openminded
- Expresses self directly, honestly, and as soon as possible about feelings and wants

- **States** things clearly
- **Checks** out other's feelings

Effects

On self:
- Increases self-esteem and self-confidence
- Has more energy
- Feels contented
- Feels good about oneself

On others:
- Increases self-esteem and self-confidence
- Feel motivated and understood
- Have high morale
- Feel listened to and acknowledged
- Know where they stand

There may be times when your assertive behavior is received in a negative way by another. This can happen because your behavior is different from what it was in the past. Some people feel threatened by any change in behavior. However, if you expect your new behavior to have a positive effect and are persistent in it, the other person will gradually become comfortable with your new behavior.

Using the assertive style assists you in making your interpersonal relationships more clear, forceful, and honest. Assertive supervisors gain respect and enhance their image as leaders. Applying the assertive approach can reduce stress, tension, and anxiety and can help you to be less preoccupied with self-consciousness and less driven by the need to control.

EXERCISE 3.4   **Practice in Assertiveness**

This exercise will give you an opportunity to practice some of the concepts discussed in the first three chapters. The following are four on-the-job situations. Write in the space provided what you think an assertive supervisor would say. Then check your responses at the end of the exercise.

1. Your boss made a derogatory remark to you. What will you say?

2. Your manager wants to pull you off a project on which you have been working for two months and give it to someone else. You think you have been doing a good job, and you want to finish it. What will you say?

3. Joe, a new employee, treats the rest of the staff critically. His remarks are affecting the morale of the group. You decide to confront him. What will you say?

4. Miriam, one of your employees, is very intelligent and sharp. She does the portion of her work she enjoys very efficiently, but she avoids tasks that she doesn't like doing. What will you say?

Discussion of Exercise 3.4

1. Suggested answer: "I want to talk to you about something that has been bothering me. I'd like to discuss the negative remarks you made to me yesterday and clarify what you meant by them so I can take corrective action."

2. Suggested answer: "I've put a lot of time and energy into this project, and I find it very interesting. I'd like to finish it. Could we discuss your reasons for wanting to take me off it and perhaps find a workable alternative?"

3. Suggested answer: "Joe, I overheard you on three or four occasions make critical remarks to Irene and Tim. [State examples.] How we communicate with each other in this work group is very important to me. I want to discuss with you how you could let Irene and Tim know what you don't like without putting them down."

4. Suggested answer: "Miriam, I have noticed that you do some of your work very effectively and, yet, let other portions of your work go undone. This puzzles me because it isn't like you not to fulfill your responsibilities. Tell me what's going on."

You may have had some trouble developing assertive statements. This will be covered in more detail in Chapter 7. The purpose of this practice exercise was to start you thinking within the assertive philosophical framework by responding to others nonjudgmentally, stating observations—rather than labeling and judging, and taking responsibility for the ways you feel and act.

SUMMARY

In this chapter, you learned the differences among the passive, aggressive, and assertive supervisory styles. You saw how the three styles fit on a continuum and how the assertive style varies, depending on the person and the situation being handled.

You saw how excessive passivity can lead to passive aggressive behavior. You also learned that the extremely aggressive style is the most dehumanizing, as it treats people as nonpersons or things. And a summarization of each style was broken down into categories that provided you with an overall behavior pattern style inventory, as well as a practice exercise to start you applying the concepts discussed in the first three chapters.

4   Unblocking Your Assertiveness to Build Your Self-Esteem

No one can get you to feel inferior without your consent.
Eleanor Roosevelt

Be what you is because if you be what you ain't then you ain't what you is.
Unknown

Knowing yourself is a significant element of being an assertive supervisor. Your primary goal is to cause individuals to work effectively as individuals and as a group to create most efficiently the specific products or services of your organization while having due regard for their own personal interests. Each supervisor has a unique way of reaching these supervisory goals based on his or her own style and personality. Thus, self-analysis is essential. Knowing yourself is a powerful tool to being successful.

DEFINITION OF SELF-ESTEEM

What is self-esteem? There are a variety of ways to define and describe *self-esteem*. The following are the essential characteristics that play a critical part in the ability of people to have a positive sense of self and high self-esteem:

- An inner knowing of one's value of goodness

- Having a vision of and commitment to one's purpose in life

- Treating oneself as one's own best friend, rather than one's own best enemy

- Knowing that each person has free will and, thus, taking charge of one's life by directing it into constructive channels

- Knowing oneself so that one can be conscious in the moment to make appropriate choices

- Accepting the reality of what is and finding a positive way to respond to life's lessons

Self-esteem plays a major part in determining which behavioral style—passive, aggressive, assertive—supervisors will use to manage their people. In order to be effective in dealing with others, it is important to accept that *you* are the most important person in your world. You can reduce the sense of inadequacy and emotional turmoil that keeps you from supervising effectively by developing sound self-esteem. You can genuinely have a high regard for others when you have a high regard for yourself and like yourself. In other words, the first order of business is to love yourself; "Love thy neighbor as thyself." It's pretty hard to love or care about others if you hate yourself. That self-hate tends to be projected unto others. It has a filtering affect on how you perceive others.

ASSESSMENT | Self-Awareness Assessment

Most people don't consciously examine how they feel about themselves. One way to determine your degree of self-esteem is by evaluating how you perceive yourself. This evaluation will give you a profile that indicates your degree of self-esteem. Score the following statements as follows:

   0   Not true
   1   Somewhat true

2　Largely true
3　True

Condition or Action	Score
1. I like myself.	_____
2. At times, I find it hard to handle situations in the way that I would like.	_____
3. I usually think others are better than I am.	_____
4. I approach life joyfully.	_____
5. I usually treat myself like I'm my own best friend.	_____
6. I usually feel open and friendly toward those with whom I interact.	_____
7. I tend to put myself down for my mistakes and shortcomings.	_____
8. I have high energy.	_____
9. I am concerned about what others think or say of me.	_____
10. I can let others make a mistake without attempting to put them in the wrong for making it.	_____
11. I feel not OK if I don't get recognition and approval.	_____
12. I feel frustrated when I don't get a task done right.	_____
13. I usually feel resentful when I lose.	_____
14. I approach something new with confidence.	_____
15. I think for myself.	_____
16. I usually take responsibility for the things I do that don't work out well.	_____
17. I don't give myself credit for my abilities and achievements.	_____
18. I know what my higher purpose is and I direct my attention to accomplishing it.	_____
19. I am afraid to let others know my real self.	_____
20. I express my feelings with ease.	_____
21. I am critical and judgmental of others.	_____
22. I take risks with confidence.	_____
23. I feel very vulnerable to others' opinions and comments.	_____
24. I usually let other people's needs come before mine.	_____

Discussion of Assessment: Self-Esteem Action Plan

Now that you have scored yourself, go back and examine your self-assessment.

1. Pick three things on the assessment that you found you like about yourself.

How do these qualities help you to be an effective supervisor?

2. Pick two things you want to improve or modify.

How would improving or modifying these qualities increase your supervisory effectiveness?

Write three things you can do to begin modifying or improving these qualities.

As many people do, you might find value in having a close friend or relative complete this assessment with you in mind. In other words, the friend or relative would score the assessment as they see you. You then compare your self-assessment with theirs. You might be surprised to discover how much more positively another sees you than you see yourself.

You can have as many people as you want do this. This can be very valuable in terms of working as well as in personal relationships, as it often enhances a sense of joy and understanding. Remember, a person's perception is his or her reality even if that perception is off mark!

One of the stages in modifying your behavior is giving yourself permission to take a risk at being or doing something different. Implicit in the risk is the understanding that you may succeed or fail; but, in either case, you develop the confidence and expertise that come from testing yourself in a responsible yet innovative way. People who take risks at work constantly surpass themselves in high performance.

Your self-esteem rises in relation to the risks you take. That's one reason assertive supervisors have a higher level of self-esteem than passive supervisors. Passive supervisors are afraid to take a chance; they don't venture, and so they don't gain in self-esteem.

GAINING CONTROL OF YOUR ENVIRONMENT

The Conditioning Process

The self-awareness assessment on page 72 gave you feedback about how you perceive yourself. Since this self-concept was largely formed in childhood, examining the conditioning process through which you lived as you grew up will help you to understand yourself better.

One way of looking at this conditioning process is to analyze how your past set the stage for your here-and-now behavior. You are socialized by your environment and your upbringing to behave and communicate in certain ways.

As part of the childhood developmental process, you incorporate into your own personality the personalities of the adults around you. This includes the numerous kinds of interactions that occur, such as how you were criticized or labeled, the kinds of messages expressed about what you should and shouldn't be, how you are given recognition and attention, how you are punished, and what kinds of feelings you are allowed to feel.

CASE Kevin had parents who withheld their love if he did things that they considered wrong. They would ignore him for hours or days until he behaved exactly as they demanded. To get them to love him again, Kevin would do anything, including being not what he was but what they wanted him to be.

In the same way, as a newly appointed supervisor, Kevin pleases others by being self-sacrificing. He feels compelled to serve others, and he expresses himself through meeting the needs of others at the expense of his own needs. Because he doesn't want to do anything for which others won't like him, he avoids confrontations and doesn't ask his employees to do distasteful tasks.

His strong need for approval and his self-sacrificing attitude resulted in his developing low self-esteem and a passive, likable behavioral style. His dread of confrontation and asking employees to do distasteful tasks led to his working ten to twelve hours a day while everyone else was going home on time.

Fortunately for Kevin and others, the habits acquired in childhood can be replaced with more positive ones by uncovering them and developing an action plan for self-improvement.

Analyzing Childhood Messages

One way to replace old, negative habits is to uncover the messages you received in childhood and then examine their effects on your adult behavior. The messages listed below are ones that many people find have the most effect on their behaving in nonassertive ways and lowering their self-esteem.

1. Place an X by those messages you feel you received as a child. Pick two to analyze in terms of their effect on your adult behavior. Then compare your analysis with the examples that follow.

_____ "Be nice!"

_____ "Don't be angry."

_____ "Don't fight back."

_____ "Grit your teeth and bear it."

_____ "Don't interrupt."

_____ "Be careful or you might get hurt."

_____ "Children should be seen and not heard."

_____ "If you can't say anything nice, then don't say anything."

_____ "Don't speak your mind."

_____ "What will other people think?"

_____ "Be perfect."

_____ "Older people know better than you."

_____ "Don't ask stupid questions."

_____ "Always finish what you start."

_____ "Don't talk back."

_____ "Don't make trouble."

2. List any other messages that are not listed in Exercise 1.

3. Pick two of the messages you received and analyze how they have affected your adult behavior.

Message	Ramifications
1.	1.
2.	2.

Discussion of Exercise 4.1

The following are some examples of messages and their ramifications.

Message to Child	Ramifications on Adult
"Children should be seen and not heard."	Doesn't speak up Is unable to express self Has low self-esteem; feels opinions are worthless
"Be perfect."	Is afraid to rock the boat Is guilty and frustrated when things aren't done perfectly Has unrealistic expectations of self and others Is never satisfied
"Don't show your anger."	Suppresses feelings Avoids people who get angry Withdraws when others are angry Tries to change own feelings
"What will other people think?"	Considers what other people think more important than own thoughts Worries about what others think Lets others be the judge Lacks self-confidence

It is our nature to be assertive. Until children are conditioned, they respond to life very assertively, asking for what they want, saying no, being persistent, and going after what they desire. Conditioned behaviors are learned as a way to survive, since the decisions we make as children aren't made with adult knowledge and understanding. However, we as adults can make decisions that are more appropriate for us in the here and now. In other words, we can unlearn old behaviors and replace them with behaviors that will aid us in being more effective. Part of the process of growth is to unravel all the programming we have acquired through the years and return to where we began.

CHANGING A NEGATIVE SELF-IMAGE

Marvin, a supervisor on a production line of twelve people, had heard over and over as a child, "Don't ask such dumb questions" and "What makes you think you know anything about that?" He was made supervisor because for years he was a first-class worker who never raised his voice and got along with everyone in the department. He didn't feel he had supervisory ability but didn't know how to turn down the promotion.

After being promoted, Marvin found his world falling apart. He disliked giving orders and couldn't face on-the-job conflicts. He couldn't bring himself to tell his employees what he thought when they voiced an opinion different from his, even though he felt he was right. He found it impossible to criticize their below-standard work—even though it was becoming more prevalent under his supervision.

His self-concept included "I'm stupid" and "I can't make decisions." Thus, he did stupid things that resulted in his staff thinking less of him, and he took a long time to make decisions, which made him seem wishy-washy.

Marvin uncovered his childhood messages while completing an exercise like the one you just did. He decided to do something about them and developed a plan of action to overcome the control they had over him. His plan consisted of the following steps:

1. Change the negative messages to positive statements; for example, "Don't ask dumb questions" can be changed to "It's OK for me to ask questions to understand better, even though they might be dumb."

2. Decide how to respond to someone saying something like "That was a dumb question"; for example, "That may be true, but asking it helped me better understand what you wanted done. I don't like making errors, and my question was a way of decreasing them."

3. Reflect on who communicates the negative messages most often, and decide how to modify the way to respond to that person.

4. Develop a "script" in order to be sure to respond according to the modified behavior.

5. Visualize the positive interaction repeatedly during free moments in order to imprint the positive image.

Marvin decided it was Dave, a supervisor from another department, who most often put him down. He decided to modify how he responded to Dave.

He thought of the last time Dave had said "That's a dumb question" to him. He developed the following "script" in order to be sure he would respond to Dave according to his modified behavior:

Script: Dave has just told me how he thinks the task that we're co-ordinating together—performance goals for first-line supervisors—should be done.

> ME: Dave, I don't understand what you mean by "ratio of jobs com-pleted on schedule to total jobs worked."
> DAVE: That's a dumb question.
> ME: It may be a dumb question, but asking it will help me to under-stand what we're doing so I can work with you more effectively. Now, what do you mean by "ratio of jobs completed on schedule to total jobs worked?"

Marvin visualized the positive interaction repeatedly whenever he had a few moments. He began to see himself as a person who could ask questions and respond assertively when someone said to him something like "That's a dumb question." Whenever he heard himself say "I shouldn't ask dumb questions," he internally stated his new affirmation to himself: "It's important for me to ask questions to understand better, even though others might think they are dumb." The critical component of this pro-cess is that Marvin listened to himself to hear the negative programming so he could replace it with his positive affirmation. (In Chapter 5, listen-ing to yourself is covered in more depth.)

Marvin was pleasantly surprised to find that he gradually became better at responding to Dave and others. He continued with the process by examining others' negative messages and modifying them in the same way. He has now changed several of them, which has resulted in his being more comfortable making decisions, stating his opinions, and telling his staff how he feels. He is now in the process of modifying how he handles conflict situations with his manager.

SELF-CONCEPT

The self-concept plays an important role in the makeup of one's personality and behavioral style. The things people say to children result in their developing a mental picture of themselves that includes all kinds of characteristics, abilities and lack of abilities, and all the things they should or shouldn't do; in other words, all the labels that are applied to them. This development of the self-concept is distorted in that children lack the control over their environment, the understanding, and the cognitive development to deal with the negative labels.

This leads to self-defeating behavior and limited self-awareness, that is, the degree of clarity with which people perceive and understand, both consciously and unconsciously, all factors that affect their lives. This awareness determines their needs and how they fill them, their behavior, how they feel toward self, how they relate to others, and their self-esteem. So, inadequate self-esteem is basically a problem in awareness. It results from minds that have been programmed or conditioned by the often distorted perceptions acquired throughout their lives, especially during childhood, that lead to the development of an ineffective behavior style.

In order to understand this issue more clearly, think of your brain as a garden. You most certainly would want your garden to grow beautiful flowers and nutritious, delicious food—flowers to nourish your spirit and nutritious food to nourish your body. The flowers and food could be related to positive, loving thoughts: A garden full of weeds would be a brain full of negative, self-defeating thoughts. On the other hand, the more positive thoughts you have, the more your garden would have nourishment for your body and spirit.

Listening to your thoughts plays a vital role in consciously growing your garden. By listening to yourself, you are in charge of what grows in your brain garden. When you consciously listen to your thoughts, you can determine if you are planting a weed, a flower, or nourishing food. The choice is yours.

EXERCISE 4.2 | **Self-Concept Attribute Checklist**

A way to assess what kind of brain/garden you are growing in terms of your self-concept is to assess it by studying this list of adjectives. You'll notice some of them are positive (flowers/nourishing foods) or negative (weeds). These adjectives identify character attributes, and most will describe you—some more than others. You are to assess your self-concept by scoring each attribute using the following scale:

3   Almost all of the time
2   Some of the time
1   Once in a while
0   Almost never

_____ accepting	_____ fearful	_____ nurturing
_____ adaptable	_____ foolish	_____ objective
_____ adventurous	_____ frank	_____ organized
_____ aggressive	_____ free	_____ overprotective
_____ anxious	_____ friendly	_____ passive
_____ authoritative	_____ gentle	_____ patient
_____ aware	_____ giving	_____ perceptive
_____ belligerent	_____ gruff	_____ perfectionistic
_____ bold	_____ guilty	_____ persistent
_____ calm	_____ gullible	_____ persuasive
_____ careless	_____ happy	_____ playful
_____ caring	_____ helpful	_____ pleasant
_____ cheerful	_____ helpless	_____ powerful
_____ clever	_____ hostile	_____ pragmatic
_____ cold	_____ idealistic	_____ precise
_____ confident	_____ imaginative	_____ progressive
_____ conforming	_____ impulsive	_____ protective
_____ controlled	_____ independent	_____ proud
_____ cranky	_____ innovative	_____ quarrelsome
_____ creative	_____ intelligent	_____ questioning
_____ critical	_____ introverted	_____ quiet
_____ curious	_____ intuitive	_____ realistic
_____ demanding	_____ irresponsible	_____ reasonable
_____ dependable	_____ irritable	_____ rebellious
_____ dependent	_____ joyful	_____ reflective
_____ determined	_____ judgmental	_____ regretful
_____ disciplined	_____ kind	_____ relaxed
_____ domineering	_____ knowledgeable	_____ reliable
_____ dutiful	_____ logical	_____ resentful
_____ effective	_____ loving	_____ reserved
_____ efficient	_____ manipulative	_____ responsible
_____ empathetic	_____ modest	_____ responsive
_____ energetic	_____ negative	_____ rigid
_____ extroverted	_____ nervous	_____ sarcastic
_____ fair	_____ noisy	_____ satisfied

_____ searching	_____ shy	_____ thoughtful
_____ self-accepting	_____ sociable	_____ trusting
_____ self-actualizing	_____ spontaneous	_____ uncertain
_____ self-assertive	_____ stable	_____ unpredictable
_____ self-aware	_____ strong	_____ warm
_____ self-conscious	_____ sympathetic	_____ wishful
_____ self-effacing	_____ tactful	_____ withdrawn
_____ self-righteous	_____ temperamental	_____ witty
_____ serious	_____ tense	_____ worried

1. Examine your assessment and note those attributes that you scored 3, "almost all of the time." Pick three or four that especially pertain to you and write them here.

   Your self-concept consists mainly of these attributes. Take a few moments to reflect on how this image of yourself as a person influences your supervisory and behavioral style—passive, aggressive, or assertive. Note your thoughts here.

   Which qualities would it benefit you to modify?

   What is one thing you can do to start modifying one of the above attributes?

2. Now repeat the process for those behaviors you scored 0, "almost never." Pick three or four on which you want to work or improve.

   Your self-concept excludes these attributes. Take a few moments to reflect on how the absence of these attributes in your self-image affects your supervisory and behavioral style. Note your thoughts here.

Which of these qualities would it benefit you to increase?

What is one thing you can do to start increasing one of the above attributes?

3. Now list ten attributes that you like and want to continue to have because they result in your being effective as a supervisor.

Some people like to express this awareness as a garden, drawing and coloring flowers or foods and identifying them as the specific positive qualities for which they scored a 3. Weeds are drawn and identified as the negative qualities for which they scored a 3. In this way, they get a visual image of their self-concept. Have fun with this. Use your imagination to draw your garden in the way from which you would get the most value.

THE OK ATTITUDES

Self-concept has another dimension: the "OKness" of self and others. People's attitude about themselves and others is a phenomenon originally explored by the late Dr. Eric Berne, author of *Games People Play.** Through his research and observations, Dr. Berne identified four life positions that manifested into these attitudes:

- I'm OK–you're OK

- I'm OK–you're not OK

- I'm not OK–you're OK

- I'm not OK–you're not OK

---

*New York: Grove Press, 1964.

Each attitude has an influence on one's feelings and behavior. Thus, supervisors with low self-esteem and a negative self-concept operate from the attitude I'm not OK–you're OK and most often in the passive style. I'm OK–you're not OK results in the aggressive style. I'm not OK–you're not OK results in swinging from passive to aggressive styles. I'm OK–you're OK results in an assertive style.

Take a moment to examine the OK circle in Figure 4.1, which gives the characteristics, behaviors, and feelings of each of the four OK attitudes. Pay particular attention to how the four attitudes relate to the three supervisory styles—assertive, passive, and aggressive.

EXERCISE 4.3

Identifying the Four OK Attitudes

Now that you've examined the four OK attitudes, it's time to practice identifying them in on-the-job situations.

In each of the following four situations, decide what attitude the person is taking. Make your notation in the space provided. After you have completed your analysis, compare your answers with those at the end of the exercise.

1. A supervisor has just discovered that a file clerk has misplaced an important report that must get out immediately. Response: "What do you mean, you can't locate the Wilson report? Can't you keep track of anything you are responsible for?"

   OK attitude: _____

2. In a weekly meeting, two employees are talking loudly to each other, while June, another employee, is summarizing the alternatives to a problem that the group is facing. The supervisor says: "I'm really sorry but, ah, I can't hear what June is saying. Do you think you could talk a little bit softer?"

   OK attitude: _____

3. A supervisor with a load of work scheduled to get out by the end of the week is asked by the general manager to take on two extra projects "as a favor to me, because you do such good work." Response: "You probably aren't aware that I presently have a heavy workload and deadlines at the end of the week. I wouldn't be able to meet my deadlines and get your work out, too. What would you like me to do?"

   OK attitude: _____

4. A supervisor has just explained a task for the third time to an employee who has been on the job over a year. The supervisor says: "You're hopeless. Damn it! I just can't explain things the right way."

   OK attitude: _____

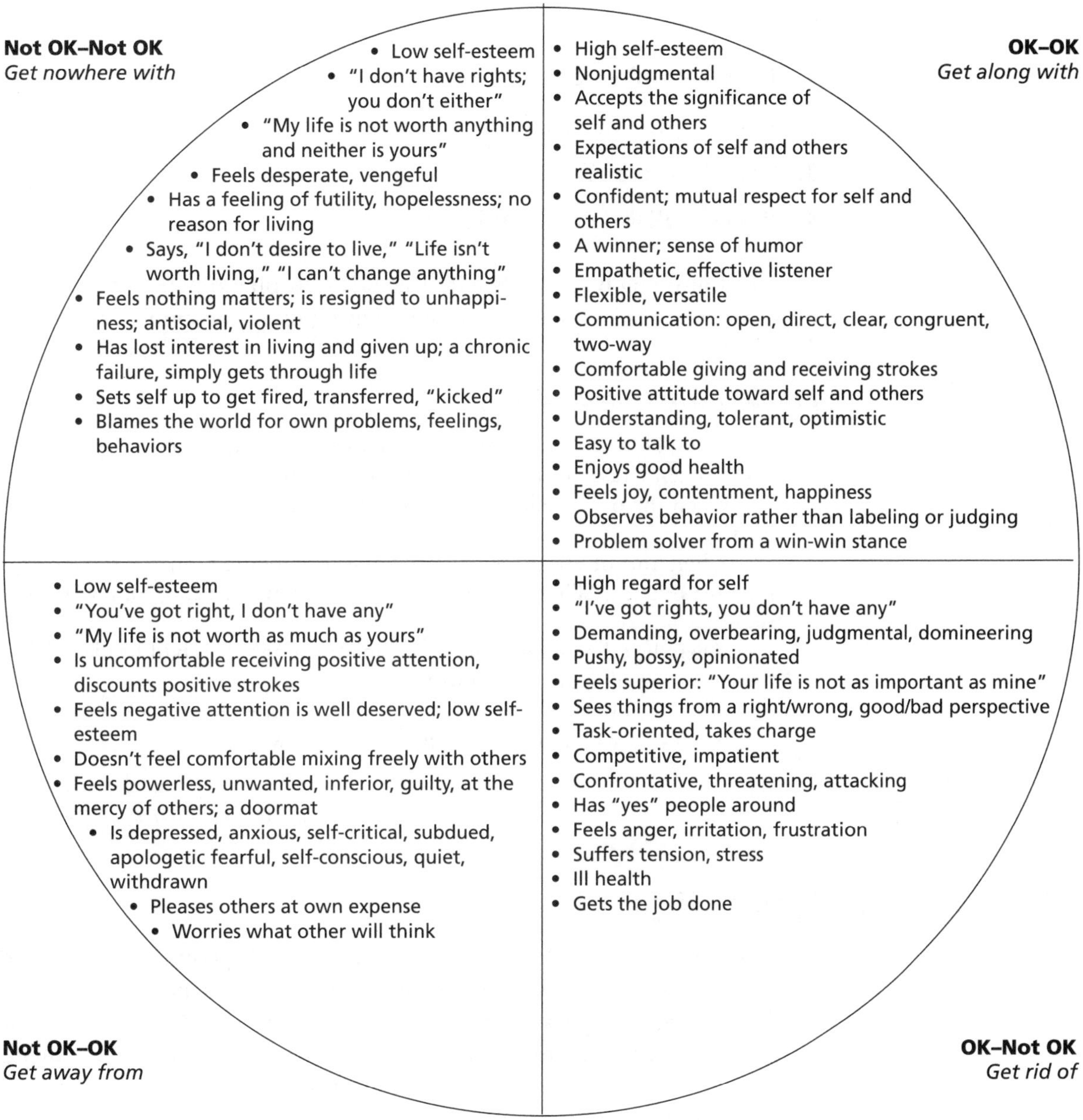

Not OK–Not OK
Get nowhere with

- Low self-esteem
- "I don't have rights; you don't either"
- "My life is not worth anything and neither is yours"
- Feels desperate, vengeful
- Has a feeling of futility, hopelessness; no reason for living
- Says, "I don't desire to live," "Life isn't worth living," "I can't change anything"
- Feels nothing matters; is resigned to unhappiness; antisocial, violent
- Has lost interest in living and given up; a chronic failure, simply gets through life
- Sets self up to get fired, transferred, "kicked"
- Blames the world for own problems, feelings, behaviors

OK–OK
Get along with

- High self-esteem
- Nonjudgmental
- Accepts the significance of self and others
- Expectations of self and others realistic
- Confident; mutual respect for self and others
- A winner; sense of humor
- Empathetic, effective listener
- Flexible, versatile
- Communication: open, direct, clear, congruent, two-way
- Comfortable giving and receiving strokes
- Positive attitude toward self and others
- Understanding, tolerant, optimistic
- Easy to talk to
- Enjoys good health
- Feels joy, contentment, happiness
- Observes behavior rather than labeling or judging
- Problem solver from a win-win stance

Not OK–OK
Get away from

- Low self-esteem
- "You've got right, I don't have any"
- "My life is not worth as much as yours"
- Is uncomfortable receiving positive attention, discounts positive strokes
- Feels negative attention is well deserved; low self-esteem
- Doesn't feel comfortable mixing freely with others
- Feels powerless, unwanted, inferior, guilty, at the mercy of others; a doormat
- Is depressed, anxious, self-critical, subdued, apologetic fearful, self-conscious, quiet, withdrawn
- Pleases others at own expense
- Worries what other will think

OK–Not OK
Get rid of

- High regard for self
- "I've got rights, you don't have any"
- Demanding, overbearing, judgmental, domineering
- Pushy, bossy, opinionated
- Feels superior: "Your life is not as important as mine"
- Sees things from a right/wrong, good/bad perspective
- Task-oriented, takes charge
- Competitive, impatient
- Confrontative, threatening, attacking
- Has "yes" people around
- Feels anger, irritation, frustration
- Suffers tension, stress
- Ill health
- Gets the job done

FIGURE 4.1
OK circle.

Answers:

1. I'm OK–you're not OK

2. I'm not OK–you're OK

3. I'm OK–you're OK

4. I'm not OK–you're not OK

The following piece deals with this OK–OK phenomenon in a human way, yet states the concept precisely, while pulling no punches.

I'm OK–You're Not OK

Isn't it funny, when the other fellow takes a long time to do something, he's slow. When I take a long time to do something, I'm thorough.

When the other fellow doesn't do it, he's lazy. When I don't do it, I'm busy.

When the other fellow does it without being told, he's overstepping his bounds. When I go ahead and do it without being told, that's initiative.

When the other fellow states his opinion strongly, he's bull-headed. When I state my opinion strongly, I'm firm.

When the other fellow overlooks a few rules of etiquette, he's rude. When I skip a few rules of etiquette, I'm doing my own thing.

by Charles McHarry
in the New York *Daily News*

THE A→B→C→D BELIEF MODEL

The importance of the OK attitudes lies in the beliefs people hold in regard to themselves and others. These beliefs influence what people value, the kind of attitudes they have, and their expectations of self and others. The end result of this mental process is how they behave and feel. In his writings, Dr. Albert Ellis* deals with this process extensively, focusing on the irrational beliefs that come from the many "shoulds," "have to's," "musts," "supposed to's," and "ought to's" that lead to a strict judgmental framework of right/wrong, bad/good. Supervisors too dominated by "shoulds" and "musts" often supervise from the extreme ends of the continuum: passive style (I'm not OK–you're OK), or aggressive style (I'm

---

*See Bibliography.

OK–you're not OK), or flip-flop from one to the other. Supervisors who are nonjudgmental and look at situations from a flexible, open-minded point of view (rather than from a strict, rigid one) are more able to supervise in the assertive style.

This is not to say that there won't be some "shoulds" in a work unit. However, employees work more productively when they are treated like adults instead of children, when they help establish the rules rather than having the rules laid on them, and when they are given credit for the work they do rather than having it ignored.

Dr. Ellis diagrams the mental process like this:

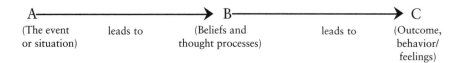

The Ellis model is modified here to include perceptions, interpretations, and the OK attitudes, because these issues are critical to understanding why people behave and feel the way they do. In addition, it shows how the OK attitudes fit into the model.

Examine how this process might work with the OK attitudes and the three supervisory styles of passive, assertive, and aggressive in regard to the same on-the-job situation.

CASE   Betty is a supervisor. Wally, an employee who is not under Betty's supervision but reports directly to her boss, repeatedly criticizes Betty in front of others, saying that she takes time off (when she doesn't) and doesn't do her job well. So far, Betty has been ignoring the situation and not saying anything to Wally. When someone repeats what he has said, she denies the accusation.

This case illustrates step A, the event. The following three examples show what could happen if Betty were to go through three different thought processes pertaining to the event. You should easily be able to identify the passive, assertive, and aggressive styles.

Example 1:

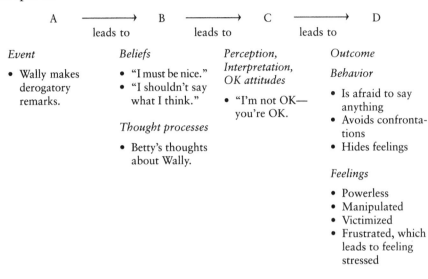

A $\longrightarrow$	B $\longrightarrow$	C $\longrightarrow$	D
leads to	leads to	leads to	

Event

- Wally makes derogatory remarks.

Beliefs

- "I must be nice."
- "I shouldn't say what I think."

Thought processes

- Betty's thoughts about Wally.

Perception, Interpretation, OK attitudes

- "I'm not OK— you're OK."

Outcome

Behavior

- Is afraid to say anything
- Avoids confrontations
- Hides feelings

Feelings

- Powerless
- Manipulated
- Victimized
- Frustrated, which leads to feeling stressed

Example 2:

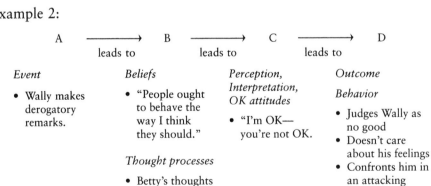

A $\longrightarrow$	B $\longrightarrow$	C $\longrightarrow$	D
leads to	leads to	leads to	

Event

- Wally makes derogatory remarks.

Beliefs

- "People ought to behave the way I think they should."

Thought processes

- Betty's thoughts about Wally.

Perception, Interpretation, OK attitudes

- "I'm OK— you're not OK."

Outcome

Behavior

- Judges Wally as no good
- Doesn't care about his feelings
- Confronts him in an attacking manner
- Blames Wally for her feelings

Feelings

- Anger
- Resentment
- Harassed

Example 3:

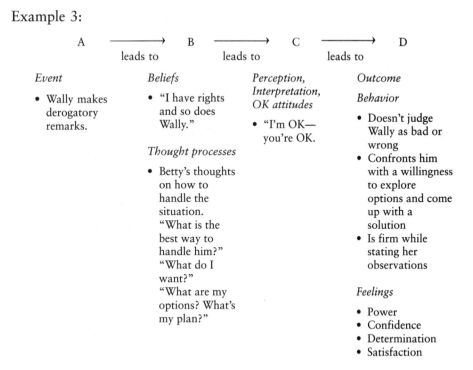

A $\xrightarrow{\text{leads to}}$ B $\xrightarrow{\text{leads to}}$ C $\xrightarrow{\text{leads to}}$ D

Event

- Wally makes derogatory remarks.

Beliefs

- "I have rights and so does Wally."

Thought processes

- Betty's thoughts on how to handle the situation. "What is the best way to handle him?" "What do I want?" "What are my options? What's my plan?"

Perception, Interpretation, OK attitudes

- "I'm OK— you're OK."

Outcome

Behavior

- Doesn't judge Wally as bad or wrong
- Confronts him with a willingness to explore options and come up with a solution
- Is firm while stating her observations

Feelings

- Power
- Confidence
- Determination
- Satisfaction

How this process affects your personal growth will be discussed in more detail in Chapter 11. However, keep the A→B→C→D belief model in mind. It will help you to be more conscious of how you block yourself from being assertive.

OBSTACLES TO HIGH SELF-ESTEEM

Irrational Fears

Irrational fears can lower your self-esteem and hinder your supervisory effectiveness. If you let inner misgivings take hold of you, you will almost surely supervise others in the passive style. Complete the following exercise to learn about the irrational fears from which you may be suffering.

Irrational Fears

Read the following list of fear statements. Put an X next to those that you think reflect the fears you have.

_____ 1. If I assert myself, something bad will happen.

_____ 2. If something bad happens, I won't be able to handle the situation.

EXERCISE 4.3

_____ 3. If I assert myself, I will be seen as selfish.

_____ 4. I will look stupid.

_____ 5. Nobody will like me; everyone will disapprove if I express my anger.

_____ 6. Others will become angry.

_____ 7. I will hurt others' feelings.

_____ 8. People will say bad things about me.

_____ 9. I'll be rebuffed or criticized.

_____ 10. I might saddle someone with too much work.

_____ 11. I don't want to cause trouble.

What will happen if you act from the fears you checked?

What could you do to overcome the fears you checked?

One way to overcome your fears is to change the fearful, negative message into a positive one, as in the following examples:

Negative Message	Positive Message
• "If I tell June she's made a mistake on the monthly report, I'll hurt her feelings."	• "June will be grateful to me for pointing out her error."
• "What right have I to disagree with the boss's decision?"	• "My boss is paying me to offer an intelligent opinion."
• "I can't risk appearing pushy by asking Jim to take on extra work today."	• "I won't be effective if I don't ask employees to take on extra work when the job has to be done to meet the deadline."
• "If I express my anger, people won't like me."	• "Anger is a natural human emotion. The way it is expressed can be either constructive or destructive."

**Rigid
Requirements**

Another obstacle to self-esteem is the rigid requirements people some-times set for themselves in terms of when they "should" assert them-selves. This is also a way to rationalize when they "shouldn't" assert themselves. The following exercise will help you become aware of this tendency in yourself.

EXERCISE 4.4

Rigid Requirements

Read the following list of statements and put a check next to any you think reflect conditions that stop you from being assertive.

_____ 1. I'll be assertive if it's important enough.

_____ 2. I'll be assertive if it happens again.

_____ 3. I'll be assertive if I have enough time to deal with it.

_____ 4. I'll be assertive if [other:]

_____ 5. If I can't deal with it, why bother?

_____ 6. I don't want to make waves.

_____ 7. I don't want to open a can of worms.

_____ 8. I'll try [without intending to do it].

What will happen if you continue to set the rigid requirements you checked?

What can you do to overcome this self-defeating behavior?

HOW LOW SELF-ESTEEM IS PERPETUATED

The following are factors that cause people to have low self-esteem and result in their feeling inadequate and frustrated.

1. Lack of faith in oneself and in a purposeful universe

2. Lack of a sense of meaning and purpose in life and, thus, a lack of clear-cut goals and objectives to motivate and guide one's decisions and endeavors, resulting in a lack of accomplishment

3. Dependence on others for a sense of importance and realness

4. Failure to accept complete responsibility for one's own life and well-being and to take full charge of one's own life and direct it into constructive channels

5. A tendency to react instead of thinking and acting for oneself

6. Failure to recognize and exercise one's innate authority to do anything one sees fit; dependence on others for what one could do for oneself; seeking the permission, confirmation, and agreement of others before acting

7. Adherence to false concepts, values, and assumptions that cause one to condemn, blame, and feel guilty

8. Failure to develop one's inherent capabilities and talents in order to make the most of one's innate potential

9. Refusal to allow oneself the right and freedom of full expression—to make mistakes, to "goof off," to fail

10. Overidentification with one's actions; failure to differentiate between "who one is" and "what one did"; indulgence in self-blame, shame, guilt, and remorse

It is important to know that your *behavior* is to be evaluated and questioned, but not *yourself. It is not possible for you to be a failure or bad.* Your behavior may be the pits . . . but not you. You can adjust your behavior if you have a positive sense of self. It is important to work with what's useful for you to do and to not get caught up in asking what's wrong and assigning blame.

POWERS OF YOUR INNER SELF

Beliefs

All of the powers of your inner self are activated by your conscious beliefs. You may have lost a sense of responsibility for your conscious thought because you have been taught that it does not form your life. You may have been told that you are terrorized by unconscious conditioning regardless of your beliefs. As long as you hold this conscious belief, you will experience it as reality.

Some of your beliefs originated in your childhood, but you are not at their mercy unless you believe that you are. Because your imagination follows your beliefs, you can find yourself in a vicious circle in which you constantly paint mental pictures that reinforce negative aspects of your life.

The imaginative events generate appropriate emotions, which automatically bring hormonal changes in your body that eventually cause disease, affect your behavior with others, and cause you to interpret events in the light of your beliefs. And so, daily experience will seem to justify what you believe more and more. Figure 4.2 illustrates this self-defeating belief cycle.

One successful way out of this cycle is to become aware of your beliefs and of your conscious thought and to then change your beliefs to bring them more in line with the kind of reality you want to experience. Imagination and emotion will then automatically come into play to reinforce the new beliefs. Figure 4.3 illustrates this positive belief cycle.

The first important step is to realize that your beliefs about reality are just that—*beliefs* about reality and not necessarily *attributes* of reality. It's important to make a clear distinction between yourself and your beliefs. It's crucial to realize that what you believe to be true in your experience *is* true. To change the effect, you must change the original belief, while being aware that, for a time, the results and effects of the old beliefs may still hold.

Your new beliefs will quickly begin to show themselves in your experience. Don't be overly concerned with their emergence, for this brings up the fear that the new ideas will not materialize, which negates your purpose.

FIGURE 4.2

Self-defeating belief cycle.

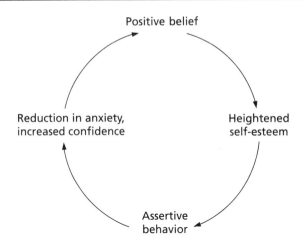

FIGURE 4.3

Positive belief cycle.

There is another dimension to your beliefs that is vital to building your self-esteem, which is your higher purpose in life. At the beginning of this chapter, I listed six essential characteristics that will help you build your self-esteem. The second one, "Having a vision of and commitment to one's purpose in life," is probably the most significant. Think for a moment of the famous people who had a vision, a commitment, and a higher purpose and who had an extraordinary impact on humanity. The founding fathers of this country are a good example. Their higher purpose was to bring to America a constitution that would allow freedoms that no other nation on this planet had ever been given. They were so dedicated to this higher purpose that they spent years researching other forms of government, constitutions, and forms of rule. They took from the teachings of other famous people, such as Cicero, Aristotle, Coke, Locke, Polybius, Solon, Montesquieu, Adam Smith, the Native Americans, and the Bible. These teachings were major influences to James Madison and Thomas Jefferson, the two main framers of the U.S. Constitution.

One of the main reasons that the Constitution has endured is that it was derived from long-established customs, beliefs, statutes, and interests. True constitutions are not invented overnight by radical philosophers. They grow instead, as if they were plants. What dedication, vision, and purpose these people demonstrated—*people,* rather than *men,* because each man was in some way influenced by a woman: a wife, a mother, a sister, or a female friend.

Think what your life might be like if these founding fathers hadn't had this higher purpose. You might be living under another country's rule, with a reduced standard of living, curtailed freedom, and lost opportunities to reach your potential or to provide for your children in a manner you can feel good about.

Once I realized my higher purpose, which is "To make the world a better place to live," my life changed dramatically. This purpose is always foremost in my mind when I have a decision to make concerning what to put my energy into. I ask myself where can I put my focus so that it will bring to fruition my higher purpose—what will have the greatest impact on the most people.

You may want to take a moment to reflect on what your higher purpose is, why are you here, and what you can do to bring the greatest good to your life and to this most wondrous planet.

Affirmations for Building Self-Esteem: Daily Action Plan

The following are some action statements that will help you affirm yourself in a positive way. You will want to say these statements to yourself while seeing a mental picture of yourself that reflects the affirmation. There are various ways you can use them. Some people, for example, have put their affirmations on 3 x 5 cards and carry them in their purse or pocket. Whenever they have some time—while waiting in line, waiting for a bus, train, or plane, and so on—they take them out and repeat them to themselves. Others have recorded them on an audio cassette and play them before going to sleep so that their dreaming minds can work on them while they are asleep. Whatever method you use, it is important that you say these affirmations to yourself daily.

This process isn't anything new. Christ said centuries ago, "As a man [person] thinketh, that's what he [or she] is." One of the basic laws of success is this: *Act as if you are going to succeed.* When you assume you will succeed, a bit of magic happens: You begin to make it possible by improving your present performance.

Affirmations

1. I have the ability to form my own experience.

2. I form the fabric of my experience through my beliefs and expectations.

3. I solve my problems and resolve my difficulties.

4. I am what I am, and I will be more.

5. I am change, and I change continually. All action is change, for otherwise the universe would be static.

6. I am understanding, and understanding flows through me.

7. I am the final authority for what I do.

8. I accept responsibility for the results of my actions.

9. I allow myself the freedom to make mistakes and to learn from them.

10. I analyze and benefit from my mistakes.

11. I am committed to my higher purpose and actively pursue it.

12. I treat myself with kindness and love.

13. Blaming others keeps me from realizing my potential.

14. I create reality through the beliefs I hold.

15. I take action to change self-defeating behavior.

16. I refuse to accept blame, shame, or guilt.

17. I give precedence to my own needs and desires as I see fit.

18. I express my needs, feelings, and opinions even if they don't please others.

19. I influence others in a positive way that encourages them to realize their potential.

20. I accept the reality of what is and find a positive way to respond to life's lessons.

SUMMARY

In this chapter, you examined the nature of self-esteem, how people acquire a positive or negative self-concept through the conditioning process, and how both affect a supervisor's style of dealing with others. You analyzed how negative childhood messages affect adult behavior and how they can be replaced with more positive ones.

You examined how self-concept influences the four OK attitudes and how they are similar to the three supervisory styles—assertive, passive, aggressive—covered in this book.

You examined the A→B→C→D belief model and how each supervisory style would handle the same situation and the different results experienced in each case.

You looked at the obstacles to developing self-esteem, such as irrational fears and rigid requirements, and how low self-esteem is perpetuated. You learned that the powers of your inner self can change self-defeating behaviors to positive ones by following a daily affirmation action plan for building your self-esteem. Finally, you explored the power in knowing what your higher purpose is. You saw how people became famous and dramatically impacted humanity because of their vision, higher purpose, and commitment to making it happen.

5   **Listening**

Nothing is quite so annoying as to have someone go right on talking when you're interrupting.

Unknown

A certain supervisor had trouble communicating with his people. Finally, in desperation, he pleaded, "Don't listen to what I say. Listen to what I mean."

Unknown

Listening is probably *the* most essential ingredient of being a success as a supervisor. The one attribute most often stated about a well-liked boss is, "He [or she] really listens to me." Supervisors who listen to their work group build rapport, swiftly clear up misunderstandings, increase respect, and build esteem in both themselves and others. As you learned in Chapter 3, a concern for human rights is a vital characteristic of the assertive supervisor. These same rights make up the framework for effective listening.

THE CARING/UNDERSTANDING ENVIRONMENT VS. THE DISTANCING/RESISTING ENVIRONMENT

Your communication style, which includes the way you listen, has a direct impact on the kind of environment you create around you. Figure

5.1 shows the behaviors that contribute to a caring/understanding environment and those that contribute to a distancing/resisting environment.

To be a better listener and to create a caring/understanding environment, you need an attitude about people that includes the following ideas:

- "I'm responsible for my actions, feelings and behavior."
- "People are fine just the way they are."
- "I don't have the power to change others, only myself."
- "Refraining from judging others will assist me in listening to them."
- "I take joy in people and value their uniqueness."
- "I allow others to be on an equal level with myself."

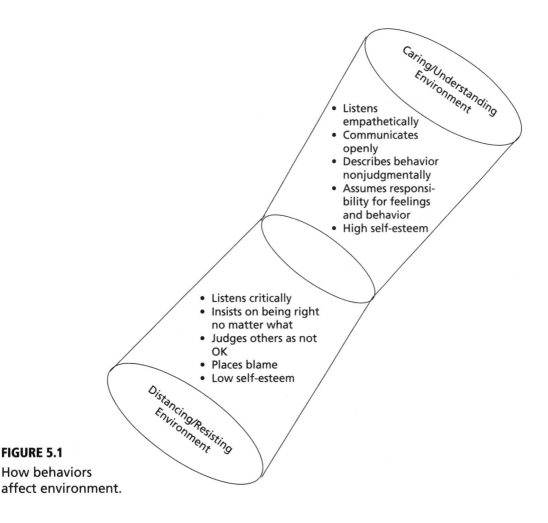

FIGURE 5.1

How behaviors affect environment.

Acquiring this kind of attitude takes concentration and commitment. It is not always easy to maintain this attitude, however your relationships will work out more successfully if you do.

Chapter 4 showed you how great an influence the past has on your present behavior. Conditioned attitudes can also interfere with effective listening as well as move you toward the distancing/resisting environment. Attitudes to shun include:

- Judging others

- Putting responsibility of how you feel and behave on others

- Trying to change others

- Believing that only a few people deserve your respect, and then only if their behavior continues to please you

- Feeling that people should do what you expect them to do and believing that there is only a right/wrong–bad/good way of looking at things.

Others will generally treat you just as you treat them. If a person is commonly critical and judgmental of others, he or she will feel that others are doing the same thing. Conversely, if one makes a habit of extending acceptance, openness, and respect toward others, one will sense that others are doing the same. In this way, one can create for oneself a world that is critical and hostile or one that is friendly and supportive.

EXERCISE 5.1   **Self-Awareness Check—Listening Behavior**

1. Take a moment to explore in more detail the messages from your past that may have conditioned you to listen poorly. The following are common early messages people receive. Put an X by those you think have influenced your present listening behavior.

_____ "Don't argue with me."

_____ "You don't know what you're talking about!"

_____ "Don't interrupt your elders."

_____ "Don't be forward."

_____ "Shut up and listen."

_____ "Children should be seen and not heard."

_____ "Be quiet."

_____ "You're too young to understand."

_____ "Open your ears!"

_____ "Don't speak until you're spoken to."

_____ "Look at me when I talk to you."

List any other messages you received that aren't listed above.

2. How have the messages that you checked influenced your present listening behavior? Use the space below to write your examples.

What can you do to modify your behavior?

3. Does your listening behavior change when you are talking to a person in authority? If so, how does it change?

What can you do to modify your behavior?

4. Do you avoid presenting an alternative view of an issue so as not to argue with the talker? If so, with whom?

What can you do to start offering your point of view?

Becoming aware of these messages can be an important step to being a better listener, as in the case of Bill.

CASE   Bill has found that the manner in which his father responded to him in childhood has had a detrimental effect on his behavior when interacting with his manager. Bill's father looked at him disapprovingly when Bill talked to him about ideas with which his father didn't agree. He would often interrupt him in the middle of a sentence to tell him he was wrong. As a result of this childhood experience, Bill had difficulty concentrating when his manager talked to him. He would worry about how he was coming across, not about what his manager was saying.

BENEFITS OF EFFECTIVE LISTENING

There are many benefits for supervisors who listen effectively to those they supervise. When employees know they are talking to a listener instead of a supervisor who sits in judgment, they openly suggest ideas and share feelings. The supervisor then has an opportunity to respond to aspects of the person's character that otherwise might have gone unnoticed.

As an effective listener, you set in motion a positive, mutually rewarding process by demonstrating interest in the employee and in what he or she is saying. This empathetic listening encourages honesty, understanding, and a feeling of security in the employee.

Listening also encourages employees to feel self-confident. This in turn can build their self-esteem and feeling of being empowered. When your employees share a problem with you, for example, do you get the sinking feeling that it is your responsibility to solve it? If so, you are probably wasting your energy. A request for listening is usually not a request for help. Therefore, your main task is to listen with understanding and nonjudgmentally. Generally, maintaining an open, available stance while seeking information and showing concern is an effective, assertive style of communicating. Your listening may be the only help required. Active listening alleviates the problem by giving the employee a chance to talk it through while experiencing emotional release. Given the opportunity to solve their own problems, employees tend to feel more confident in their abilities.

Employees who are listened to will not bottle up their feelings. Thus, listening is a potent force for reducing stress and tension. Listening tells the employee, "Your feelings are legitimate." Conversely, employees who are not listened to get the message that their feelings are not important. Holding feelings in does not get rid of them. Sooner or later, they will erupt, probably in a negative form, such as missing deadlines, being late for work, or not putting in extra effort to get the job done.

CASE   Terry, a supervisor, was sitting in his office when Geri, one of his better employees, came charging in looking angry. In an abrupt manner, she exclaimed, "Terry, I don't like the way things are handled around here. I don't feel you are being fair. I feel I am being taken advantage of!"

Terry's first impulse was to snap back defensively, "What do you mean? You don't know what you're talking about. I don't do that!" Instead, he stopped himself, put aside what he was working on, took a deep breath, and gave Geri his full attention.

"You sound upset about something I've done. Tell me what's happened."

"First of all, it seems to me that just because I'm a good and fast worker I get penalized for it. Whenever you want something done, I'm the first one who gets it, no matter how much work I have to do!"

Terry had a strong urge to snap back a rebuttal, but he didn't. He concentrated on listening to the feelings behind Geri's words and responded, "I can understand how you might feel. Tell me more."

"Well," continued Geri, "I got back from my break, and there was a whole pile of new work on my desk that you evidently put there for me to do . . . no explanation, no nothing!"

"Geri, " replied Terry, "I'm puzzled by what you're saying. You're right—I did put that work on your desk—but I also put a note on top of it that said for you to come see me when you got back so that I could explain to you what the work was all about. Didn't you see the note?"

Looking somewhat taken aback, Geri said haltingly, "Uh, no . . . I didn't see one."

"Well, maybe it blew off your desk," suggested Terry. "It probably would have been better for me to take it to you in person instead of leaving it on your desk."

By listening with understanding and remaining objective, Terry was able to stop himself from responding defensively to Geri, thus preventing an angry encounter between the two of them. Terry's listening skill is one of the major reasons he is successful in dealing with conflict. He has found that how he responds to others has a definite influence on how they respond to him.

Terry has discovered that the real challenge is in adjusting his communication style to get the response that leads to problem solving and a positive result.

LISTENING IS A SKILL

As a method of communication, listening is used far more than reading and writing combined. Ironically, it is the least understood function of all. When thinking about listening, most people tend to assume it is basically the same as hearing—a dangerous misconception that leads to believing that effective listening is instinctive. As a result, people make little effort to learn or develop listening skills and unknowingly neglect a vital communication function.

Of all the time spent communicating, by far the greatest is spent in listening. Figure 5.2 shows how the communication process breaks down. You may not have realized that listening is such an important skill.

One manager who was curious about how much time he spent listening asked his secretary to keep track of the time he spent listening on the telephone. He was shocked to discover that his company was paying him 25% of his salary for this function alone, or $8,000.

Amazingly, on the average, people are only about 25% effective as listeners. If this manager's listening skill is at the 25% efficiency rate, he is paid about $13,500 for listening *ineffectively!**

EXERCISE 5.2   ## Listening Evaluation**

The following evaluation will give you an idea of the listening habits for which you can pat yourself on the back and those habits you might want to reshape.

Listening: The Forgotten Skill, Madelyn Burley-Allen (New York: John Wiley and Sons, 1982).
**Taken from *Listening: The Forgotten Skill*, a prepackaged program developed and published by Dynamics of Human Behavior, San Mateo, CA (1992).

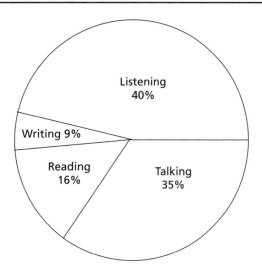

FIGURE 5.2

How people communicate.
From studies summarized by Dr. Ralph Nichols in his book *Are You LIstening?* (New York: McGraw Hill, 1957).

Answer each question thoughtfully by imagining yourself on the job. How do you generally respond to people in these situations—not the way you should or would like to, but the way you actually do? Put an X in the appropriate column that represents how often you do that behavior.

Communicating knowledge and attitudes	Most of the time	Frequently	Occasionally	Almost never
Do you:				
1. Tune out people who say something you don't want to hear or with which you don't agree?				
2. Concentrate on what is being said, even if you are not really interested?				
3. Assume you know what the talker is going to say and stop listening?				
4. Repeat in your own words what the talker has just said?				

Communicating knowledge and attitudes	Most of the time	Frequently	Occasionally	Almost never
Do you:				
5. Listen to the other person's viewpoint, even if it differs from yours?				
6. Learn something from each person you meet, even if it is slight?				
7. Find out what words mean when they are not familiar to you?				
8. Form a rebuttal in your head while the talker is speaking?				
9. Give the appearance of being an effective listener when you're not listening to a word that's being said?				
10. Daydream while the talker is speaking?				
11. Listen to the whole message—what the talker is saying verbally and nonverbally?				
12. Recognize that words don't always mean exactly the same thing to different people?				
13. Listen only to what you want to hear, blotting out the rest of the message?				
14. Look at the person who is talking?				

Communicating knowledge and attitudes	Most of the time	Frequently	Occasionally	Almost never
Do you:				
15. Concentrate on the talker's meaning rather than on how he or she looks?				
16. Know which words and phrases tend to make you emotional?				
17. Think about what you want to accomplish with your communication?				
18. Plan the best time to say what you want to say?				
19. Think about how the other person might react to what you say?				
20. Consider the best way (written, spoken, phone, bulletin board, memo, etc.) to make your communication work?				
21. Think about what kind of person you're talking to (worried, hostile, disinterested, rushed, shy, stubborn, impatient, etc.)?				
22. Interrupt the talker while he or she is still talking?				
23. Think "I assume he or she would know that"?				

Communicating knowledge and attitudes	Most of the time	Frequently	Occasionally	Almost never
Do you:				
24. Allow the talker to vent negative feelings toward you without becoming defensive?				
25. Practice regularly to increase your listening efficiency?				
26. Take notes when necessary to help you remember?				
27. Let sounds distract you?				
28. Listen to the talker without judging or criticizing?				
29. Restate instructions and messages to be sure you understand correctly?				
30. Paraphrase what you believe the talker is feeling?				

Discussion of Exercise 5.2

To score this exercise, circle the number that represents the category you checked on each item of the self-evaluation. Add the circled numbers to obtain your total score.

	Most of the time	Frequently	Occa- sionally	Almost never		Most of the time	Frequently	Occa- sionally	Almost never
1.	1	2	3	4	16.	4	3	2	1
2.	4	3	2	1	17.	4	3	2	1
3.	1	2	3	4	18.	4	3	2	1
4.	4	3	2	1	19.	4	3	2	1
5.	4	3	2	1	20.	4	3	2	1
6.	4	3	2	1	21.	4	3	2	1
7.	4	3	2	1	22.	1	2	3	4
8.	1	2	3	4	23.	1	2	3	4
9	1	2	3	4	24.	4	3	2	1
10.	1	2	3	4	25.	4	3	2	1
11.	4	3	2	1	26.	4	3	2	1
12.	4	3	2	1	27.	1	2	3	4
13.	1	2	3	4	28.	4	3	2	1
14.	4	3	2	1	29.	4	3	2	1
15.	4	3	2	1	30.	4	3	2	1

TOTAL _____

Rating: 105–120 Superior
89–104 Above average
73–88 Average
57–72 Fair

Reexamine your responses. Identify three behaviors that you want to modify and/or improve. In the space given, state one thing you could do to improve or modify each of these behaviors.

1.

2.

3.

HOW OK ATTITUDES AFFECT LISTENING STYLES

Supervisors with the aggressive "I'm OK–you're not OK" style tend not to listen. They are most often busy being critical and judgmental, forming rebuttals internally, interrupting, and only half-listening. They have the attitude, "Why bother listening to not-OK people? They don't have anything worthwhile to say anyway."

CASE   Greg's father's style of listening matched the aggressive "I'm OK–you're not OK" listening style. As a supervisor in a large federal agency, Greg adopted many of his father's listening behaviors. As a result, his employees don't feel that he listens to them. They often complain that Greg listens with a critical expression on his face. He quickly judges and criticizes what they have to say. And he seems to listen only to what he has to say, as if he is the only one with good ideas. When someone brings up an opposing point of view, Greg hears what he wants to hear, filtering out comments with which he doesn't agree. His aggressive manner and listening style often leave people feeling stupid. Thus, Greg listens much the same as his father did, not realizing that his behavior is affecting others negatively.

On the other hand, supervisors with the passive "I'm not OK–you're OK" style are busy concentrating on themselves. Their feelings of not-OKness result in a negative attitude that interferes with their paying full attention to what the talker is saying.

CASE   Kathy has a passive "I'm not OK–you're OK" supervisory style. Her behavior is very different from Greg's. She often worries about how she is coming across, focusing on herself rather than on the dynamics of what is going on between herself and others.
During meetings, she is reluctant to speak up because she believes that what she has to say will be stupid. She often says, "I'll probably say something dumb anyway, so why bother?" Because she listens passively, she only half listens.

Assertive supervisors have a significant edge over passive and aggressive supervisors. Supervisors who listen earn the respect and loyality of their work group and discover important things about the business. One company hired an expensive management consultant to find out why the workers showed signs of low morale. The consultant sought the cause of dissatisfaction using a method the company's managers could have used themselves. He directly asked the workers why they were unhappy—and listened to their answers. Within a short period of time, he knew exactly why morale was low.

IMPROVED PRODUCTIVITY

Employees frequently have excellent ideas about improving productivity and the work environment. Supervisors who listen for these ideas solve more problems than those who do not.

CASE   One day, Ted, a supervisor, called his lead man, Jim, into his office to explain his plans for a new way to assemble machinery. He described how he thought the procedure should be changed. Jim's only response was silence and a frown. Ted realized something was wrong and sensed Jim might have something to say.

"Jim," he began, "you've been in the department longer than I have. What's your reaction to my suggestion? I'm listening."

Jim paused and then began to speak. He realized his supervisor had opened the door to communication and, so, felt comfortable offering suggestions from his years of experience. As the two men exchanged ideas, a mutual respect and trust developed, along with a solution to the technical problem of the changeover.

Listening is one of the most positive ways a supervisor can "stroke" an employee, since everyone likes recognition and attention. Like Jim, people who are listened to leave the encounter feeling valued and important. This builds self-esteem. For instance, when a secretary suddenly begins to make typing errors, mumbles under her breath, and snaps at a co-worker, a boss who is listening may say something like, "You seem upset about something. Are you?" To be listened to can make one feel understood and worthwhile as a human being. On the other hand, if the boss had been critical—"You shouldn't lose your temper and snap at people!"—the secretary, who is already feeling out of sorts, may take his critical comment as a real putdown.

THE IMPORTANCE OF LISTENING TO NONVERBAL COMMUNICATION

People can also stroke one another by the way they "listen" to nonverbal communication. A listener may turn a talker off by a certain look, a shift to a closed posture, or impatient foot tapping. When you listen with an attentive look, lean forward with interest, and maintain an open body posture, you communicate nonverbally in a positive way. Much is communication that isn't verbalized!

Recent studies reveal three major categories through which communication is conveyed. They are shown in the following table. For each category, circle the percentage number that you think represents the correct part of the whole communication process.

	Relative Impact (Approximate)			
Words (verbal)	30%	7%	16%	42%
Vocal (tone)	40%	27%	38%	10%
Facial expressions, posture, gestures, and eye contact (nonverbal)	20%	55%	32%	40%

Did you guess correctly? The figures of 7% for words, 38% for vocal (tone of voice), and 55% for facial expressions posture, gestures, and eye contact were quoted in a widely read article by Albert Mehrabain.* Another prominent authority, Randall Harrison, claimed that a mere 35% of the meaning of a communication comes from words; the remainder comes from body language.** You may question the specific percentages reached by these researchers, but you probably don't dispute the general direction of their findings. Nonverbal expression is, indeed, significant in the listening process. Think for a moment of the times people have influenced you simply by the way they looked at you.

It is interesting to note that Americans like eye contact. Surveys taken by the author during seminars have revealed that Americans like about 60% eye contact during a communication, but they don't like to be stared at! People say they suspect that people who don't look them in the eye are trying to hide something. After all, the "eyes are the windows of the soul." Eyes tell things about a person, and people like to "read" eyes.

This desire for eye contact isn't true for some Eastern cultures, Native Americans, and some districts in large U.S. cities. In fact, in some Asian cultures, it is disrespectful to look people in the eyes, especially when talking to a person in authority. My seminar participants in Singapore, Malaysia, and Indonesia have confirmed this belief over and over again, and they talk about how different they are in this respect to Americans.

---

*"Communication Without Words," *Psychology Today*, September 1968, p. 53.
**"Nonverbal Communication: Exploration into Time, Space, Action, and Object," *Dimensions in Communication*, eds. James Campbell and Hall Hepner (Belmont, CA: Wadsworth, 1970), p. 258.

Close observation will reveal how much people convey through facial expressions. Watch facial color and how it changes as people refer to things about which they have strong feelings. Movements of the lips, mouth, cheek, muscles, and eyebrows can reveal a lot about what is going on inside the person to whom you are listening. Become aware of expressions that convey tension, doubt, trust, inattention, and so forth.

Listening to the emotional tone of a speaker is another important skill. The tone of voice can convey attitudes that can provide a clue as to how to deal with a person in a difficult situation. Skilled listeners listen to the pitch, rate, timber, and subtle variations of the speaker's tone of voice. One manager says that when an employee enters her office, she often asks herself, "What does the voice say when I stop listening to the words and listen only to the tone and inflection?" In the dynamics of the communication process, people can affect others without saying a word.

EXERCISE 5.3	**Nonverbal Communication**

Take a moment to reflect on the following questions and write your responses.

How do people let you know nonverbally that

1. they aren't listening?

2. they have a problem?

3. they want to terminate the conversation?

4. they aren't interested in what is being said?

5. they have responded to "red flag" words?

6. they are daydreaming?

Now examine your answers. Do any of them describe *your* behavior? If there is any behavior you want to change, write a plan for how you could begin to modify or change your behavior. If you found some things about yourself that you like, pat yourself on the back.

Plan of Action to Change Behavior:

Things You Like about Yourself:

LEVELS OF LISTENING

Listening can be divided into three levels that are characterized by certain behaviors that affect listening efficiency. These levels are not sharply distinct but rather general categories into which people fall; they may overlap or interchange, depending on what is happening. As a person moves from level 3 to level 1, the potential for understanding, retention, and effective communication increases. People listen at different levels of efficiency throughout the day, depending on the circumstances and the person(s) involved. Most often, people have difficulty listening effectively when in a conflict situation; when dealing with emotional people; when having criticism directed at them; when being disciplined; or when feeling anxious, fearful, or angry. Others listen effectively on the job but tune out when they get home.

The following descriptions of the three levels will help you understand the ways you listen.

Three Levels of Listening

Level 1: Empathetic listening. At this level, listeners refrain from evaluating the talker's words and place themselves in the other's position, attempting to see things from his or her point of view. Some characteristics of this level include taking in main ideas; acknowledging and responding; not letting oneself be distracted; paying attention to the talker's total communication, including body language; being empathetic to the talker's feelings and thoughts; and suspending one's own thoughts and feelings to give attention solely to listening. Empathetic listening requires an OK-OK attitude. It also requires that the listener show, both verbally and nonverbally, that he or she is truly listening.

Level 2: Hearing words, but not really listening. At this level, people stay at the surface of the communication and do not listen to the deeper meanings of what is being said. They try to hear what the talker is saying but make little effort to understand the talker's intent. Level 2 listeners tend to listen logically, being concerned about content more than feeling, and remain emotionally detached from the conversation. Level 2 listening can lead to dangerous misunderstandings because the listener is concentrating only slightly on what is said. At level 3, it is obvious that the person is not listening; however, at level 2, the talker may be lulled into a false sense of being listened to and understood.

Level 3: Listening in spurts. At this level, people tune in and tune out, being somewhat aware of others, but mainly paying attention to themselves. They follow the discussion only enough to get a chance to talk. Level 3 listening is quiet, passive listening without responding. Often a person listening at this level is faking attention while thinking about unrelated matters, forming rebuttals or advice, or preparing what he or she wants to say next. The listener may display a blank stare and is more interested in talking than listening.

Most people listen at all three levels during the course of a day. However, the more we can learn to listen at level 1, the more effective we can become in working with others.

| **EXERCISE 5.4** | **Self-Awareness Check—The Three Listening Levels** |

Think for a moment about your day.

1. How often did you listen at level 1?

   When?

   With whom?

2. How often did you listen at level 2?

   When?

   With whom?

3. How often did you listen at level 3?

   When?

With whom?

4. Develop action steps to improve your listening by completing the following two action statements.

In the area of listening, I want to:

In the area of work, what I want to accomplish through listening is:

Levels of Other Communication

These three levels are part of the whole human existence. They aren't just activated during listening. How often have you been reading a book and gotten to the bottom of the page only to find that you didn't remember anything that you read? Level 3 reading! How many memos, policies, or procedures are read at level 3? Maybe you have reached the bottom of a page and gotten the words, but you didn't understand what the author meant—level 2 reading. If you reached the bottom of a page and understood completely what the author wrote, then you were reading at level 1.

These levels also operate when people talk. Do you know anyone that talks at level 3? He or she can't tell you what they said after they finished talking and aren't aware of how much "air time" they are taking or how they are affecting the person who is listening to them. It is difficult for a level 3 talker to effectively respond to a listener's behavior. When at level 3, people have no idea of the dynamics of the communication, the cause and effect principle—how what they do causes the effects people realize in their lives.

How many people do you know that live their lives at level 3, unconscious most of the time? They make the same mistakes over and over again because they aren't aware enough to overcome them—they are tuned out of life. Then there are others who have a surface understanding of themselves and others, in and out of awareness—level 2 living.

Level 1 people have a deep understanding of themselves and others. They have taken the time and energy to become aware of who they are, how their family and cultural background influences who they are. "Know thyself" is the key to happiness and success. It's the assertive supervisor who will reap these rewards.

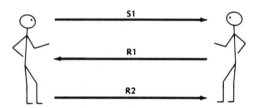

FIGURE 5.3

The empathetic listening interaction.

(Stimulus)   S1:   Person makes a statement about his problem.
(Response)   R1:   You listen and respond to the person's problem, which becomes a stimulus for
              R2:   The other person's response to your response.

EMPATHETIC LISTENING (LEVEL 1 LISTENING)

It was pointed out earlier in this chapter that the meaning of any communication is the response that it elicits. Being able to adjust your behavior style in order to change the way an interaction is going can help you deal effectively with a variety of difficult situations.

Crucial times for a supervisor to be an effective level 1 listener include when an employee is discussing a problem or expressing strong feelings, during a performance review, when resolving a disagreement between two employees, and when presenting your ideas to management. The ways you listen and respond to people in these kinds of situations will strongly influence how the problems are resolved, how the others involved will respond to you, and how they will feel about your response. Figure 5.3 shows what the interaction would look like.

Most supervisors' results are accomplished through person-to-person communication. A major function that allows you to be successful in doing this is your ability to facilitate openness and understanding with those you supervise. It is largely by your people contacts that you influence and motivate those you supervise.

Many supervisors have found the empathetic listening approach a powerful tool for improving their people skills. This approach sets into motion a supportive communication chain in which the employee feels more accepted and can be more open. The active/empathetic listening mode can be a big step in making listening work for you.

CASE   Carl, a manager for a large manufacturing company, had this to say about the power of active listening at level 1:
"Improving my listening skills has been a major reason why I have advanced in my career and become successful at working with people. My increased ability

to listen at level 1 has had several positive results and has improved personal relationships. My manner of supervising others is different than it used to be. My effective listening encourages the employee to discuss with me the negative things that are going on. By doing this, we are able to solve the problems, thus reducing the amount of negative energy expanded by the employee. I have consciously worked at listening, and I find the negative interactions I used to have at performance-appraisal time are almost eliminated.

"In the past, when I had a difficult person to deal with, I was quick to judge and be critical, which moved me into listening levels 2 and 3. I found myself forming rebuttals and thinking that the person was not OK. Now, I'm aware of when I *start* to get into this mental process, and I stop myself. I then concentrate on what's being communicated beyond the words and force myself into the OK-OK assertive mode by asking myself: What's going on that I'm being negative about? Why am I reacting this way? What can I do to listen nonjudgmentally?

"What's interesting is that my improved listening skills have influenced other parts of my behavior. Before I knew about the levels of listening, I used to think I understood what was said to me. I would misunderstand assignments given to me, and, when I was corrected for doing them inaccurately, I would blame the other person. I now perform my job more efficiently, and the amount of work I complete is increased. Needless to say, I feel better at the end of the day.

"I used to have a difficult time dealing with a key manager in the corporate headquarters. But when I made a point of listening beyond his gruff manner and often critical facial expression, I discovered I let these mannerisms move me into the I'm-not-OK passive mode. Forcing myself not to quickly judge him didn't come easy. I stayed with it. At the beginning, I could find only a couple of ways to react to him positively. After what seemed to be forever, I was able to discuss my feelings with him.

"The final result is that working with him is now bearable, and it's getting better all the time."

Keep two important ideas in mind when interacting with others: (1) people prefer talking to people who listen to them at level 1, and (2) the listener actually controls the conversation by how he or she responds nonverbally to the talker. To listen effectively and to be in control of what is being said, check your understanding regularly by summarizing what the other has said. Then wait for feedback—either confirmation that your understanding is correct or clarification of what the talker intended.

YES, BUT . . .

A supervisor is sometimes confronted with someone who has a closed mind, which often results in the "Yes, but . . ." interaction. This type of interaction can be frustrating; however, the summarizing and feeling check

SYSTEMATIC APPROACH TO EMPATHETIC LISTENING:
WAYS THE LISTENER CAN BE IN CONTROL

Objective	Method	Listening Response
I. *Clarifying Check* 1. To clarify. 2. To gather more facts. 3. To check the talker's meaning.	State a *what, how,* or *when* question; then restate what you thought you heard.	1. "Is this the problem as you see it?" 2. "Will you clarify what you mean by . . . ?" 3. "What specifically do you mean by . . . ?" 4. "What I understand you to say is. . . . Is that right?"
II. *Accuracy Check* 1. To check your listening accuracy. 2. To encourage further discussion. 3. To let the speaker know you grasp the facts.	Restate the speaker's basic ideas, emphasizing the facts.	1. "As I understand it, the problem is. . . . Am I hearing you correctly?" 2. "What I think you said was . . ."
III. *Feeling Check* 1. To show you are listening and understanding. 2. To reduce anxiety, anger, or other negative feelings. 3. To let the talker know you under-stand how he or she feels.	Reflect the talker's feelings, paraphrased in your own words. Match talker's depth of meaning, light or serious.	1. "You feel that you didn't get the proper treatment." 2. "It was unjust as you perceived it." 3. "It's annoying to have this happen to you." 4. "It seems to me that you got turned off when your boss talked to you in that angry manner." 5. "My sense is that you like doing the job but are not sure how to go about it."
IV. *Summarizing Check* 1. To focus the discussion in order to lead to a new level of discussion. 2. To focus on main points. 3. To offer a spring-board for further consideration. 4. To review progress.	Restate, reflect, and summarize major ideas and feelings.	1. "These are the key elements of the problem." 2. "Let's see now, we've examined these factors . . ." 3. "These seem to be the key ideas you express . . ." 4. "To summarize, the main points as I heard them are . . ."

SYSTEMATIC APPROACH TO EMPATHETIC LISTENING *(continued)*

Objective	Method	Listening Response
V. *Noncommittal Acknow-* *ledgment* 1. To stay neutral yet show you are interested. 2. To encourage and to keep a talker speaking.	Don't agree or disagree. Use noncommittal words with positive tone of voice.	1. "I see . . ." 2. "Uh-huh . . ." 3. "Mm-hmm . . ." 4. "I get the idea . . . I understand." (Silence during the pause.)
VI. *Acknowledgment of* *Problem*	Statement that there is a problem.	1. "Tell me about it." 2. "That does seem to present a problem."

can be used to deal with the problem. The following dialogue example reflects how Kent, talking to another supervisor, handled the situation before using the empathetic listening approach.

> GARY: "I just don't know what I'm going to do about my boss. He's always picking on me for little things I do wrong."
> KENT: "You should talk to him about why you're upset."
> GARY: "Yeah, but I couldn't do that. He'd make life miserable for me."
> KENT: "Well, you ought to ignore him and not let him bother you."
> GARY: "Yeah, but then I'd be letting him get away with his lousy behavior and he'd never change."
> KENT: "Well . . . you should quit and get another job."
> GARY: "Yeah, but I need the money, and the way the job market is these days, I probably wouldn't be able to find another job for months."
> KENT (by this time completely exasperated): "Why don't you get a water pistol and shoot him!"

Notice that each time Kent came up with a solution, Gary spent his listening time thinking of rebuttals to what Kent was suggesting, zeroing in on what wouldn't work. Instead of being open to Kent's suggestions, Gary used his listening time to think of reasons why he couldn't use them. This listening pattern is often perceived as going around in circles. The problem doesn't get resolved, and the person providing the solutions feels discouraged. Now see what happens when Kent uses the summarizing and listening check techniques:

GARY: "I just don't know what I'm going to do about my boss. He's always picking on me for little things I do wrong."

KENT: "Sounds like you don't know how to handle your boss when he points out things you do that he doesn't like."

GARY: "Yeah, and he does it a lot. I don't want to tell him about it because it might make him mad. Then he'd probably make life miserable for me."

KENT: "Hmmm. Seems like you're caught in a double bind. On the one hand, you want to tell your boss what you don't like, and, on the other hand, you don't want to tell him because he might get upset with you."

GARY: "Yeah, that's exactly how I feel."

KENT: "It's a tough spot to be in. What kind of choices do you have? Let's talk about them."

Notice that Kent's summarizing of what Gary said led to agreement on what was happening, in contrast to the preceding example where Gary and Kent disagreed. It also helped Gary see more clearly what was going on between him and his boss.

By being an effective listener, Kent stayed out of the "Yes, but" trap. Kent and Gary have not solved Gary's problem, but at least they have made progress toward a solution.

The following is another example of how the empathetic technique can keep the lines of communication open in order for problem solving to occur.

CLAY: "Harry, I'm really frustrated about the way things are going on the job. They just don't go the way I expect them to. Worst of all, it seems like you're never around anymore."

HARRY: "Seems like a couple of things are happening that you're not satisfied with. Tell me more."

CLAY: "Well, we're a week behind in production, and supplies aren't coming in on time. I'm feeling swamped and unable to catch up. And when I've tried to find you lately to talk to you about getting some extra help, you're off somewhere or other."

HARRY: "Sounds like you feel you're alone on a deserted island, and, when you want to talk to me, I'm not around."

CLAY: "That's right. I don't know how you expect me to do all of this by myself. Waiting two or three days to discuss things with you just doesn't work out."

HARRY: "It appears to me, Clay, that the main problem is your not being able to get in touch with me when you have a problem to work out. If I was around more, the other problems could be resolved. Is that right?"

CLAY: "That's it. I've even been wondering if you really give a damn about us making production goals or not."

HARRY: "I understand. I don't blame you for thinking that. Let's take some time right now to find ways to resolve the situation."

You'll notice that Harry responded to Clay's feelings while restating the problem in his own words. As he continued to do this, he moved the interaction toward a problem-solving action plan.

EXERCISE 5.5 **Listening Practice**

The following situations will give you a chance to practice identifying empathetic responses. For each situation, circle the response that you think is empathetic. Check your answers at the end of the exercise.

1. "It happens every time the manager appears in my department. He just takes over as if I wasn't there. When he sees something he doesn't like, he tells the employee what to do and how to do it. The employees get confused, and I get upset. What can I do?"

   A. "You should discuss your problems with your boss."

   B. "When did this start to happen?"

   C. "The boss must be the boss, I suppose, and we all have to learn to live with it."

   D. "It upsets you that your manager takes over and gives conflicting directions. You're not sure what would be the most appropriate way to confront him about your feelings regarding his behavior."

2. "It's happened again! I was describing an office problem to my boss when she started staring out the window. She doesn't seem to be really listening to me because she has to ask me to repeat things. I feel she's superficially giving me the time to state my problems, but she ends up sidestepping the issue."

   A. "You should stop talking when you feel she's not listening to you. That way, she'll start paying attention to you."

   B. "It's frustrating to have your boss behave that way when you're talking about problems that are important for you to solve."

    C. "What kinds of problems do you talk to her about?"

    D. "You can't expect her to listen to every problem you have. Anyway, you should learn to solve your own problems."

3. "I think I'm doing all right, but I don't know where I stand. I'm not sure what my manager expects of me, and he doesn't tell me how I'm doing. I'm trying my best, but I wish I knew where I stood."

    A. "Has your boss ever given you any indication of what he thinks of your work?"

    B. "If I were you, I'd discuss it with him."

    C. "Perhaps others are also in the same position. Don't let it bother you."

    D. "Not knowing if you're satisfying your boss leaves you feeling unsure, and you'd like to know just what he expects from you."

4. "He used to be one of the guys until he was promoted. Now he's not my friend anymore. I don't mind being told about my mistakes, but he doesn't have to do it in front of my co-workers. Whenever I get a chance, he's going to get his!"

    A. "To be told about your mistakes in front of co-workers is embarrassing, especially by a supervisor you once worked with."

    B. "If you didn't make so many mistakes, your boss wouldn't have to tell you about them."

    C. "Why don't you talk it over with a few people who knew him before and then go talk to him about this situation?"

    D. "How often does he do this?"

Answers: 1. D   2. B   3. D   4. A

GUIDELINES FOR EFFECTIVE LISTENING

1. Avoid being critical and judgmental as this usually increases the emotional level of the talker, making him or her feel put down and not-OK.

2. Listen to the underlying meaning of what is said. This style of listening helps build acceptance, trust, and rapport, and talkers solve their own problems. Keep in mind that you don't have to agree with what the talker is saying to be an empathetic listener—only empathetic with his or her feelings.

3. Hold any questions you may have until you have listened at level 1. Sometimes an empathetic response is necessary two or three times before the talker's emotional level has lessened to the point where he or she can think objectively and listen at level 1. By helping the person bring his or her emotional level down, the listener helps the talker be logical and analytic.

4. Refrain from trying to solve the talker's problem or to do the thinking for her or him. People feel more self-confident when they can solve their own problems. Although giving advice can make you feel needed and important, it inhibits the talker's personal and professional development.

EXERCISE 5.6   **Empathetic Listening Practice**

By following the empathetic listening approach, design listening statements in response to the following situations. Compare your responses with those at the end of the exercise.

1. Marie, a fellow supervisor who is conscientious and strong-willed, has lost the ambition to be productive. She responds irritably to routine problems and, as a result, has become difficult to work with. You are talking to her during a coffee break when she says to you: "Nobody cares. There are no efforts being made to improve conditions. We get no information or leadership from management, and we seem to have the same problems over and over."

Your response:

2. You are a supervisor of machinists. One of them, Derek, is outspoken, fault finding, and demanding. His co-workers respond to him by being offended and avoiding him as much as possible. Derek says to you: "The people who work with me are lazy and unfriendly. I tell them what they ought to do, but they don't listen to me."

Your response:

3. A fellow supervisor who is conscientious and responsible says to you in an angry voice: "I don't know how to deal with this program manager. He doesn't seem to listen to me when I tell him I'm not able to meet the date for his requested action. He knows I have to operate within state regulations, and yet he won't accept my reasons for why the action cannot be accomplished."

Your response:

Discussion of Exercise 5.6

Here are some possible empathetic responses:

1. "You seem to feel discouraged about the way things are being handled and are fed up with the same old problems."

2. "If I understand you correctly, Derek, your co-workers don't do things the way you feel they should. How do you let them know what you want them to do?"

3. "It's frustrating to feel you have explained these state regulations in an understandable way to a manager who doesn't seem to listen to how you are restricted."

HABITS TO IMPROVE YOUR LISTENING

Being an effective listener takes practice and commitment. You can practice these habits each time you're talking to someone or at a meeting. By following these 12 habits, you will improve your listening skill.

1. *Find areas of common interest.* If you adopt a positive attitude toward the topic, you will normally find something in any talk that will broaden your knowledge. Finding elements of personal value is one area of effective listening. Ask yourself: What is being said that I can use? What's in it for me? How does this relate to what I already know?

2. *Take the initiative.* Find out what the talker knows. Look at the talker and concentrate on what he or she says. Go all the way in making the communication two-way. If necessary, ignore his appearance and his

personality to reach for the idea he is conveying. Stimulate the talker by your attentiveness and expressions of interest, including noncommittal acknowledgments such as "Oh, I see," "How about that," "Mm-hmm," "Interesting," "Really," and "You did?"

3. *Work at listening.* Efficient listening takes energy. Practice will make it easier. Listen actively and energetically.

4. *Focus your attention on ideas.* Listen for the talker's central ideas. Pick out the ideas as they are stated, sorting the facts from assumptions, ideas from examples, and evidence from opinion.

5. *Hold your rebuttal: Watch out for hot buttons.* Don't let emotional words throw you. Learn to recognize words that affect you to the point where you stop listening and instead start forming a rebuttal or making a decision. Quickly analyze the reasons these words stir you, then resume listening, withholding any evaluation until you fully comprehend the point the talker is making.

6. *Keep an open mind.* Quick or violent disagreement with the talker's main points or arguments can cause a psychological blind spot. Keep your mind open. Give the talker *more* rather than less attention, searching for the full kernel of the theme. Instead of judging what the person says as wrong, clarify meaning by restating in your own words what you thought was said.

7. *Capitalize on the speed of thought by summarizing.* The core of effective listening is the development of the utmost concentration in the immediate listening situation. Most individuals talk at only 150 words per minute, yet think about three times faster. That extra thinking time can be used to concentrate on what the talker is saying. Summarize in your head what the talker has said. Decide how well he is supporting his points and how you would have supported them. Mentally review, after each point is covered, the progress of the theme. Draw contrasts and comparisons, and identify the talker's use of evidence.

8. *Practice regularly.* Get experience and practice in listening by listening to difficult or unfamiliar material that challenges your mental capacities. Every meeting should present many opportunities for practice. Regular practice will work wonders for you.

9. *Analyze what is being said nonverbally.* Be sensitive to the feelings of the talker. Ask yourself, "Why did the talker say that, and what did

he or she mean?" Listen between the lines for hidden meanings. What is the person saying nonverbally?

10. *Evaluate the talker's content, not the manner of appearance.* The talker's message is more important than his or her appearance. Don't let the talker's poor voice, mannerisms, personality, or appearance get in the way of the message.

SUMMARY

In this chapter, you learned how vital effective listening is to successfully carrying out your job as supervisor. You examined how an accepting attitude toward others can create a caring/understanding environment, whereas a rigid, critical attitude can create a distancing/resisting environment. You analyzed how childhood messages pertaining to listening affect present listening behavior. The numerous benefits of skillful listening were covered: improved productivity, enhanced team work, high morale, and others.

The characteristics of the three levels of listening were described. The importance of the empathetic listening approach to effectively handling problems was emphasized. You completed several practice exercises to aid you in incorporating this technique into your style of supervising. Finally, you were given 12 habits to practice that will aid you in being a more proficient listener.

6   **Taking Risks**

Failures are divided into two classes: those who thought and never did, and those who did and never thought.

Unknown

A wise person learns from the mistakes of others. Nobody lives long enough to make them all by himself or herself.

Unknown

Three of the most important variables that influence supervision in any organization are:

- The supervisor and his or her personality

- The employees and their personalities

- The nature of the situation

The relationship between these factors is shown in Figure 6.1.

In preceding chapters, the importance of self-analysis has been emphasized to help you become aware of your capabilities and people skills. A careful evaluation of your behavioral style will help you tailor your style to the needs of the organization and the people with whom you work.

Risk taking, the third building block of managing assertively, is a significant factor in your ability to deal with the other two variables—

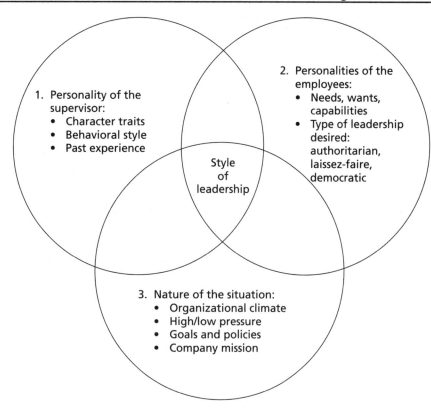

FIGURE 6.1

Three factors that affect leadership style.

employee personalities and needs and the nature of the organization. As the supervisor, you are the dynamic force in the actual work of the organization in your department or unit. You may or may not have a strong effect on things in the organization, but you are affected by everything in the organization insofar as your activities are concerned.

Risk taking is tied to self-esteem and self-confidence. If you feel good about yourself, you'll be able to take risks because you will be optimistic about their consequences. If you feel apprehensive about yourself, you will most likely be afraid to trust your own judgment.

Knowing where and how to take risks is one of the most important skills in assertive supervision. Each time you make plans and decisions, ask for what you want, state your opinions and limits, delegate a task, or suggest a course of action, you are taking a risk: The plan may not work, the decision may be incorrect, your opinion may be rejected, and the task may be done badly. This chapter will concentrate on various areas in which supervisors need to take risks.

ASKING FOR WHAT YOU WANT

Managing assertively entails feeling comfortable about asking for what you want. However, most supervisors have a difficult time doing this. When they examine why, they find it is because of childhood messages (e.g., "It's not OK to ask for what you want because you are being pushy") or hidden messages conveyed nonverbally (e.g., "Others should be able to read your mind; don't ask—wait, or they'll be annoyed"). In response, these supervisors learned to avoid the issue at hand or to deal with it indirectly, while feeling pangs of anxiety that they won't get what they want—and most often, they don't! To uncover these self-defeating messages, complete the following self-awareness check.

EXERCISE 6.1

Self-Awareness Check: Asking for What You Want

To find out if asking for what you want is an issue with which you need to deal, respond to the following statements and questions.

1. During the past few weeks, was there a time when you wanted to ask for something and didn't? Describe the event.

2. Reflect on your reasons for not asking for something you wanted. Apply to that event the A→B→C→D belief model from Chapter 4 (see page 86).

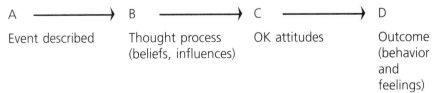

A. Event described in 1

B. Thought process (beliefs, influences)

C. OK attitude

D. Outcome (behavior and feelings)

3. Now that you are aware of the beliefs and/or messages that motivated you *not* to ask, how can you modify your thought process to help you ask the next time?

4. What action steps could you take to handle the situation more effectively the next time?

Asking Assertively for What You Want

Harold, an office manager, illustrates how passively asking for what you want usually doesn't work.

> HAROLD (looking down at the floor): "Susan, I can't seem to find anyone to take care of the photocopying and collating of next year's goal projections." (Apologetically) "I don't think it will take too long. I really would appreciate your taking care of it."
> (Harold walks away with a relieved feeling. But later that day . . .)
> HAROLD: "Oh, Susan, did you get that report completed for me?"
> SUSAN: "No, I'm sorry, Harold. I was going to take care of it, but something else came up and I didn't get around to it. Besides, from what you said, it didn't seem that important that I do it right away."

When asking for what you want, keep these guidelines in mind:

1. Make sure your choice of words is appropriate; be specific and concise.

2. Make your nonverbal behavior match your words.

3. Keep your emotional level congruent to the situation.

4. Know specifically what you want, how you want it done, when you want it, and why. Whenever possible, give others a choice as to when they can get the task done.

5. If necessary, write your request down.

6. State what you want or don't want using phrases such as:

"I want you to/I'd like you to _____ by _____ because _____."
                              (what)   (when)   (why)

"I don't want you to _____ because _____."
                      (what)   (why)

"Could/Would/Will you _____ by _____ because _____?"
                       (what)   (when)   (why)

7. Stick to the point. Provide only the information that contributes directly to what you are asking.

8. Avoid comments that do not contribute to an understanding of what you want.

EXERCISE 6.2

Following the guidelines just given, write Harold's request in a form that is more effective. Then check your revision against the possible answer.

HAROLD:

Possible Answer:

HAROLD (With good eye contact, a direct and straightforward expression, and a moderate but firm tone): "Susan, the photocopying and collating for next year's goal projections aren't done yet. They need to be done by 4 p.m. so I can take them to my meeting with Mr. Jones. This project is very important, so I'd like you to do it even if it means delaying what you are now working on. Thanks. I appreciate your help on this."

Passive Mode

Asking for a Raise

One of the most common but difficult steps people take throughout their working careers is asking for a raise.

The following is a description of how people in the passive, aggressive, and assertive modes would handle this request for a raise.

Passive: The passive person would not be prepared, wouldn't have a plan of action, and wouldn't know specifically how much of a raise she wants. She probably hasn't selected the best time to approach her manager and shuffles into her manager's office with downcast eyes. She might look uncomfortably at the floor, shift her weight from side to side, and keep her hands clasped. In a soft tone of voice she'd say, "I'm sorry to bother you, but I've been meaning to talk to you. You probably didn't notice how hard I've been working, but I have . . . and, hmmm . . . I really need a raise." Her eyes, tone of voice, mannerisms, and choice of words say to her boss, "I don't deserve a raise, and I'm not even sure I should be asking for one." Her delivery undermines her own cause.

Aggressive Mode

Assertive Mode

Aggressive: The aggressive person doesn't have a plan or gather information to support her requests; after all, she deserves the raise, so why should she bother? She doesn't consider timing. She charges into the manager's office and demands: "I deserve a raise! After all, I work harder than anyone else around here. I'd better get one, or I'll be looking elsewhere."

Assertive: The assertive person is prepared. She has gathered the facts necessary to support her request; she knows how much money she wants and she has developed what she is going to say and how she will say it. She picks the day of the week and time of day that will be best to get a positive response from her boss.

She walks confidently into her manager's office and looks at him directly. Her expression says, "I'm entitled to be paid what I am worth, and I expect to be taken seriously." She says, "Thank you for giving me the time to meet with you today. I have reviewed my pay schedule and the tasks for which I am responsible, and I feel I deserve a raise. I've noted my reasons for this request and would be happy to go over them with you. Then I'd like to discuss an amount that we feel would be fair."

While there is no guarantee that the assertive person will get her raise, the way she handles the situation can maximize her chances. Using the assertive approach increases the chances that the manager will listen. The aggressive approach usually turns the other person off, and the passive approach usually encourages the other to be critical of what is being said.

You Don't Always Get What You Want

It's not the purpose of assertive supervision to always get your way. Realistically, that's not possible. When you ask for what you want effectively, however, you will get information about what is possible.

CASE   Alex, the supervisor of the computer projects division of a medium-size company, needed a new staff member to handle the work load in his unit. He had gathered all the facts to support his request for this additional person. However, when Alex presented his plan to his manager, he said no, even though he was empathetic and interested. He had to balance Alex's request against the needs of the unit. The money in the budget was needed for a higher priority item.

Alex did not get his employee, but he did get clear information about the realistic possibilities. He also let his manager know that he wanted his request to be considered when more money was available.

Asserting yourself to ask for what you want will leave you feeling better, even if you don't get it. What is important is that you handled the situation effectively and can look back on it feeling confident that you did the best you could. Expressing your wants also helps relieve pent-up feelings and stress.

EXERCISE 6.3	**Application—Asking for What You Want**

The following are common situations in which supervisors need to ask for help. Using the guidelines discussed on pages 131–132, develop "wanting statements" to be used in each of these situations. When you are finished, compare your statements with the suggested answers that follow.

1. You are hard-pressed to get a project out. It is due tomorrow. The project is important because it is part of a joint project with three other departments. How will you ask Jeanne, your assistant, to help you out?

2. While you are giving instructions to Paul, one of your employees, he interrupts you three times. What will you say to Paul to stop the interrupting?

3. You must ask Carol to work overtime for the third time this week. You have an unexpected assignment: a price quote for a big job that came in yesterday. The company could make a healthy profit if it wins this contract. What will you say to Carol?

4. You have been in your job for five years and have been taking courses for professional development. You feel you should be promoted. You want to bring up the matter with your manager, Marvin. What will you say to him?

Possible Answers:

1. "Jeanne, I have a project to complete that will take about two hours of your time and needs to get out by tomorrow. It's part of a project that includes three other departments, and they need our contribution tomorrow. Would you have time to get it done by 10 A.M. tomorrow?"

    (If Jeanne has time, you state your appreciation. If Jeanne says she doesn't have time, then examine her work load with her to see what she is doing that has a lower priority and could be delayed in order to get your project done. Then state your appreciation.)

2. "Paul, when you interrupt me I'm not able to complete what I'm saying. You can be assured that, when I'm finished, we will go over the areas about which you have questions. How do you think we could handle this?" (Get Paul's feedback and, together, work out a plan.)

3. "Carol, I've just received an unexpected assignment. It is a quote for a big job that we received yesterday, and it has to go out in today's last mail. I appreciate your willingness to work overtime, but, quite frankly, I don't like asking you to do it three times in one week. I estimate this job will take you one hour past quitting time. Will you stay and get it done?"

    (If Carol says yes, state your appreciation. If Carol says no, then negotiate with her a reward that she values for staying overtime, such as a two-hour lunch, coming in two hours later in the morning, or leaving two hours early on Friday. Let her come up with these suggestions, as they will be more meaningful to her.)

4. "Marvin, I want to talk to you about my possibilities for promotion. I've been on the job now for five years with a good track record, along with taking courses for professional development. This promotion is important to me. When could we get together to formulate a career plan for this promotion? I have time tomorrow afternoon at 2:30 or Wednesday morning at 11:00. Would either of those times work for you?" (If neither time fits into Marvin's schedule, ask him to suggest a time.)

Speaking Up and Asking for Information

Two important functions of your job are getting the information you need to get the job done and expressing your opinions as to the best way to do it. Supervisors are reluctant to do both because of early conditioning that results in their holding back ideas and being afraid to ask for information they want and need. They restrain their natural tendencies to express what they think and what they need—to their own disadvantage!

It is important to risk speaking your mind, even though you may fear the reaction you might get. Assertive supervisors know that those in authority will benefit from what they have to say. They know they have a right to their ideas and expect others to listen to them. In other words, a supervisor using the assertive approach won't automatically defer to the boss. They know that by taking the initiative, the supervisor can often speed up the completion of a project, prevent errors, and save time.

CASE Annette, a sales analysis supervisor at a toy company, needed information from Mr. Thomas, a sales manager, to finish a project. Annette was trying to analyze the successes and failures of the fall pre-Christmas sales campaign and felt she needed to understand the sales manager's rationale for the campaign. Annette saw many inconsistencies in sales but, on her own, could only get a partial picture of what had happened.

Annette felt anxiety and fear about approaching Mr. Thomas to get the information she needed. She examined why she had these fears by following the A→B→C→D belief model. Then she took steps to overcome them by developing a plan of action and visualizing her plan in effect.

She set up a meeting with Mr. Thomas to review the numbers and what had happened on the store shelves the year before. Had Annette succumbed to her qualms about asking for information from an authority, she would have spent weeks in research and might never have come up with an answer—while all the time the needed information was right at hand.

EXERCISE 6.4

Self-Awareness Check—Speaking Up and Asking Questions

To find out if expressing your opinions or asking for information is an issue with which you need to deal, respond to the following statements and questions.

1. During the past few weeks, was there a time when you wanted to express your opinions or ask for needed information and didn't? Describe the situation.

Reflect on your reasons for not asking, applying the A→B→C→D belief model from Chapter 4 (see page 86).

A		B		C		D
Event described	→	Thought process (beliefs, influences)	→	OK attitudes	→	Outcome (behavior and feelings)

2. Now that you are aware of the beliefs and/or messages that motivated you not to express your opinion or ask for information, how can you modify your thought process to help you ask the next time?

What action steps can you take to handle the situation more effectively the next time?

KEEP YOUR THINKING STRAIGHT

When expressing your opinions or asking for information, it's important to keep your thinking straight. Some supervisors will express opinions without bothering to get the facts or supporting evidence and, so, lose credibility. They also state assumptions thinking they are facts. Supervisors often feel that getting the facts is too time consuming and that they can move faster without them.

Facts vs. Assumptions

Clearly differentiating between facts and assumptions will help you keep your thinking straight. The following table will help you examine the difference.

Facts	Assumptions
• Are specific concrete statements made about events you see going on around you.	• Are ideas added to observations; guesses about the unknown based on the known.
• Must follow observation.	• Can be made at any time.
• Approach certainty.	• Have a high or low degree of probability.
• Are limited in number.	• Are unlimited in number.
• Lead to agreement.	• Lead to disagreement.

EXERCISE 6.5

The Holmes Listening Assumption Check

Everyone makes assumptions, and there is nothing wrong with you if you do. However, it is important to be aware of how you make them. The purpose of this exercise is to demonstrate how your beliefs and assumptions affect how you interpret information. Follow the instructions given.

1. Read the following passage about the Southern Electronics Company through once. After you have finished reading it, cover it so that you are not tempted to refer to it as you respond to the statements that follow.

Story on the Southern Electronics Company

Jim Holmes, the research director of Southern Electronics Company, ordered a crash program to develop a new process. He gave three of his executives authority to spend up to $50,000 each without consulting him. He sent one of his best men, Ed O'Reilly, to the firm's West Coast plant with orders to work on the new process independently. Within one week, O'Reilly produced a highly promising new approach to the problem.

2. Respond to the following 11 statements. If what you read in the passage makes the statement true or false, circle T or F, respectively. If there wasn't enough information in the passage for you to know if the statement is true or false, then circle ?. Base your answers only on information explicitly stated in the passage.

Statements

1. Holmes sent one of his best men to the West Coast.	T	F	?
2. Holmes overestimated O'Reilly's competence.	T	F	?
3. O'Reilly failed to produce anything new.	T	F	?
4. O'Reilly lacked authority to spend money without consulting Holmes.	T	F	?
5. Only three of Holmes' executives had authority to spend money without consulting him.	T	F	?
6. The research director sent one of his best men to the firm's West Coast plant.	T	F	?
7. Three men were given authority to spend up to $50,000 each without consulting Holmes.	T	F	?
8. Holmes had a high opinion of O'Reilly.	T	F	?
9. Only four people are referred to in the passage.	T	F	?
10. O'Reilly is mentioned as the research director of an electronics firm.	T	F	?
11. While Holmes gave authority to three of his best men to spend up to $50,000, the story does not make clear whether O'Reilly was one of these men.	T	F	?

Adapted from "Listening: Sharpening Your Analytical Skills," a prepacked module, authored by Axel Freudmann, published by Training House, Inc., 100 Bear Brook Rd., Princeton Junction, N.J. 08550, 1977.

Discussion of Exercise 6.5

Now check your answers against the ones below. Score one point for each correct answer.

Answers:

1. T—That's what the passage says.

2. ?—The story doesn't say whether he did or not.

3. F—The story says he did produce something new.

4. ?—The story does not say whether or not O'Reilly had authority to spend money.

5. ?—The story does not say whether others besides the three mentioned had such authority.

6. T—That's what the passage says.

7. ?—Not all executives are necessarily men.

8. ?—The story suggests this but doesn't state it.

9. ?—If O'Reilly is one of the three executives given authority to spend $50,000, this would be true; but the passage does not specify whether he was one of the three.

10. F—Holmes was the research director.

11. T—The story does not specify whether Holmes gave such authority to his best men.

This exercise tested your ability to separate facts from assumptions. How well did you do?

Thousands of people have taken this exercise. Most people average six correct answers. It is a valuable exercise because it vividly points out how easy it is to make assumptions.

It is not always possible to state your opinions based only on facts, but it is crucial to do so whenever possible. Assertive supervisors know that relying on facts will influence others to have more confidence in their conclusions while establishing an image of someone who knows what he or she is talking about.

Guidelines for Separating Facts from Assumptions

1. *Define terms.* It's important to define not only your own opinions but also those expressed by others. Get into the habit of specifying precisely any information you receive. If, for example, someone says, "I don't see any reason for hiring accounting services from an outside firm—the price would be too high, and, even though they'd give faster service, I don't think it would be worth it," you might ask the following questions to define more clearly what the person meant:

   • Which accounting firms are being considered?

   • Exactly what makes up each firm's services?

   • How much is "too high"?

   • How fast is "faster service"?

   • What makes it "not worth it"?

   • How important is the issue—how much does it matter?

2. *Think in terms of continuity.* Look at most matters in terms of a continuum rather than in categories of this-or-that, right-or-wrong, should-or-should-not, black-or-white, yes-or-no. Many people find it frustrating when questions aren't answered in either-or terms, even though the best way to do a task often lies somewhere between the extremes. Work on breaking this habit. If, for instance, someone says that "alternating office work will eliminate waste," you could ask:

   • How is *waste* defined?

   • Can this idea be partly so and partly not so?

   • Would it be true for some tasks and not for others?

   • Would it be true for some departments and not for others?

3. *Suspend judgment.* One of the most common problems when listening to others' opinions is quickly judging or criticizing what they are saying. As you learned in Chapter 5, this is one of the most detrimental habits to effective listening. Another habit that causes difficulty is prejudging an idea or option based on a generalization. This happens when a person supports an opinion by generalizing from a single case. If, for example, someone says, "College graduates wouldn't last long in that routine job, we had one in our office and . . ." or "An elderly person couldn't handle the pressure of that position; I knew an older man who worked here some time ago and . . .." Evaluate each idea on

its individual merits rather than prejudging from a generalization. If someone did make a generalization like the examples given, you could ask a clarifying question, such as:

- How do you know *this* college graduate or older person would have a problem?

- Are you saying that because one person you knew had this problem, everybody that is a college graduate or an older person would have the problem, too?

- That might have been true for the person you knew. How do you know it's true for *this* person?

4. *Stay objective.* You can reduce subjectivity concerning opinions by asking yourself:

- How much?

- How often?

- When?

- Where?

- As compared to what?

Then go a step further and ask yourself *How important is it?* and *How much does it matter to the issue on hand?* People often pay too much attention to meaningless things that they have been conditioned to feel are important. *Don't major in the minors!*

5. *Be open-minded.* It's easy to listen to opinions with which you agree or to people you like. As a result, even the most valid idea from a person you don't like is rejected. Avoid the mistake of judging opinions or information based on feelings about their source.

SETTING LIMITS

Assertive supervisors have found that getting their work group involved in setting clear, realistic limits goes a long way toward reducing tardiness, getting tasks completed on time, improving teamwork, and helping workers view their jobs as worthwhile and enjoyable. When limits are not established because of a passive supervisory style, the outcome is broken rules, overstepping of bounds, loss of respect, supervisors feeling taken advantage of, and employees viewing supervisors as wishy-washy.

On the other hand, when limits are set arbitrarily and unrealistically by aggressive supervisors, employees often feel they are being treated unfairly, taken advantage of, and treated as children.

As you might guess, this kind of treatment results in high turnover, loss of good employees, low morale, uncooperativeness, and an unfriendly place in which to work. The assertive supervisory approach promotes an open, available stance by the supervisor, who actively seeks information on which to base conclusions.

EXERCISE 6.6   **Self-Awareness Check–Response Style Assessment**

The following assessment is designed to help you evaluate how others respond to you. It will aid you in determining how you "come across" to your employees. On the line next to each statement, write the number that best indicates how that statement applies to you.

3   Often
2   Sometimes
1   Seldom
0   Never

_____ 1. When an employee breaks an established limit, you confront the employee by finding out his or her reasons and working out a solution so it doesn't happen again.

_____ 2. At times, people draw away from you or fail to make eye contact; they seem edgy or nervous.

_____ 3. People state their opinions to you openly.

_____ 4. People move in and dominate you because they feel you won't stand up for your rights.

_____ 5. People tend to dismiss your ideas or fail to seek out your opinions.

_____ 6. At times, people seem to have more of a chip on their shoulders with you than when dealing with others.

_____ 7. When dealing with you, people sometimes become careful, tentative, and guarded.

_____ 8. People try to avoid you because they don't want to feel guilty or uncomfortable as a result of your apologetic or self-pitying behavior.

_____ 9. When you say you will help people to get what they want, they believe you.

_____ 10. People respect your opinion.

_____ 11. People rarely disagree with you and avoid crossing you.

_____ 12. People rarely ask you to take on the tough tasks in dealing with people because you are too easygoing.

_____ 13. People become condescending or patronizing because they are afraid to confront you directly; they feel you can't take it.

_____ 14. Your employees come to you when they have a problem to work out.

_____ 15. People do not bring their problems or questions to you.

_____ 16. People try to put you down or embarrass you with humor or subtle contempt.

_____ 17. Your unit is the one to which employees from other departments want to transfer.

_____ 18. People feel they can break the rules and get away with it, and you won't say anything.

Adapted from _Assertive-Responsive Management: A Personal Handbook_ by Malcolm E. Shaw (Belmont, CA: Addison-Wesley, 1985).

Discussion of Exercise 6.6

Add up your score as follows:

Numbers 1, 3, 9, 10, 14, and 17 are _assertive_ responsive statements. Write your total score for these numbered statements on the line below.

Numbers 4, 5, 8, 12, 13, and 18 are _passive_ responsive statements. Write your total score for these numbered statements on the line below.

Numbers 2, 6, 7, 11, 15, and 16 are _aggressive_ responsive statements. Write your score for these numbered statements on the line below.

Total: _____ _____ _____
                 Assertive   Passive   Aggressive

Although these response behaviors by others may be the result of their own needs, your score can help you to be more aware of others' reactions to you. Observing how others treat you can help you determine what you can do to be more effective in your dealings with them.

If your assertive score was high, there is a good chance that people will come to you with their problems, feel comfortable confronting you when they disagree, listen to your ideas, and generally want to work in your unit in a cooperative way.

If your aggressive score was high, you probably need to examine the manner in which you establish rules. It may mean you are using the theory X style of supervision discussed in Chapter 2. You might want to reflect on how your behavior is influencing your effectiveness.

If your passive score was high, it may mean that you are using theory Y style to your disadvantage. Being people oriented is a fine quality. Any strength can become a weakness when it is misused or abused. This can result in a loss of respect from those who work with you.

Establishing Limits

How you establish limits will strongly influence how they are responded to and carried out. A common problem with supervisors is that they often don't tell their staff what their limits are! They expect their employees to read their minds and to automatically do what they want them to do without being told. This results in limits not being respected and the supervisor's feeling anger, frustration, or bitterness while blaming employees for not meeting expectations. A major quality of an assertive supervisor is being responsible for what he or she wants. That means that a supervisor must let others know what the limits are.

If you are having trouble with some of your employees not meeting your limits and expectations, it is probably because you haven't discussed your limits openly and specifically. If so, establish your limits by following these guidelines:

1. Depending on the number you supervise, call a meeting or talk to each person individually.

2. Announce that you are concerned about certain limits that are being infringed upon and that you feel partly responsible for this because you haven't been clear and specific about your limits. Follow the assertive approach by using the full range of assertive behavior: words that are clear and specific, nonverbal communication that is straightforward and direct; good eye contact; and tone that is firm but not critical.

   • Have a plan (write it down, if necessary) and follow it.

   • Avoid putdowns, and withhold judgment—stay in OK–OK position.

   • Give information—examples of the behaviors with which you are concerned.

   • Express limits and/or goals.

   • Point out benefits to the group as a whole.

   • Point out negative consequences to the work group.

3. Tell the group that you want to set up a time when all of you can meet to explore alternatives for dealing with the situation. You want to give them time to think about the concerns you expressed and about ways to deal with them. The objective of the meeting will be twofold:

   • Establishment of limits so that things run smoothly.

   • Resolution of problems that interfere with observance of these limits.

4. Emphasize that employees will have an opportunity to express their gripes, needs, and ideas. If they choose not to express them, they are responsible for not getting their needs or wants met. Also, give those who are uncomfortable stating things publicly an opportunity to express their needs in written form. They may hand them in in an unmarked envelope. Assure their anonymity. Establish a deadline for written requests to be handed in.

5. Schedule the meeting at a time during the day when it will cause the least difficulty. You might have the employees decide when the best time will be.

EXERCISE 6.7   ## Practice—Setting Limits

To practice setting limits is useful. Design assertive statements in response to each of the following situations. Then compare your statements with the possible answers that follow.

1. One of your employees, Ben, has been late for the third time during the past two weeks. You haven't said anything to him before because he is a valuable employee and is usually on time. On the other hand, you don't want this lateness to continue. You've decided to confront him and state your limits about being on time. What will you say?

2. Sarah, one of your employees, does her work thoroughly and with very few errors. However, she often doesn't complete them on time, which results in deadlines not being met. The other workers, who depend on her to get their work completed, are feeling frustrated. You've decided it's time to confront her and work out a solution. What will you say?

Possible Answers:

1. "Ben, I noticed that you were 10 minutes late three times during last week and this week. (Facts are stated, yet judgment is withheld). This lateness is not like you—you are usually on time. (His timeliness is acknowledged.) What happened to cause you to be late?" (Feedback is requested. Say there was difficulty with the public transportation system he uses.) "Ben, I can now understand why you were late. In the future, when this happens, I'd like you to let me know so that I don't make faulty assumptions about your lateness."

2. "Sarah, I want to talk to you about the length of time it takes you to complete your tasks. (Facts are stated without putdowns.) I have hesitated to do so because your work is done thoroughly and with very few errors. (Positive feedback is given.) However, it has become an issue because your rate is affecting deadlines and others are feeling frustrated. (Negative consequences are spelled out.) I want to meet deadlines and have a happy work group. (Goal and want are stated.) If I allow you to continue your present speed, this won't happen. What do you think can be done to resolve this issue?" (Input is requested on how issue could be resolved.)

SUMMARY

This chapter covered the three most important variables that influence supervision:

- The supervisor and his or her personality
- The employees and their personalities
- The nature of the situation

You learned that it is important to take risks by asking for what you want, by letting your staff know what your limits and expectations are, by speaking up to get the information you want, by stating your ideas, and by delegating work. You examined how a supervisor would handle these risk-taking situations in each of the three supervisory styles—assertive, passive, and aggressive. Beliefs and assumptions were discussed that interfere with your stating your wants and limits and with your getting the information needed to do the job properly. Guidelines for you to use in stating your wants and limits were given. You completed practice exercises that will aid you in handling on-the-job situations that could cause difficulty.

7 Constructive Feedback: Criticism

One may find the faults of others in a few minutes, while it takes a lifetime to discover one's own.

Unknown

Judging others is a dangerous thing; not so much because you may make mistakes about them but because you may be revealing the truth about yourself.

Unknown

The art of being wise is the art of knowing what to overlook.

William James

The word *criticism* has a negative connotation. This is the reason "Constructive Feedback" precedes "Criticism" in this chapter title. Criticism, the fourth building block of assertive supervision, seems to cause a great deal of discomfort to both those giving the feedback and those receiving it. When criticisms are given in a judgmental, unfavorable, I'm OK–you're-not-OK, aggressive style, no wonder people feel negative!

Passive supervisors find correcting employees a disagreeable job. This results in their dodging it until pressure builds up, and they finally blow their tops and express the criticism harshly and from the aggressive behavior mode.

These passive supervisors are doing their employees a disservice by failing to call attention to problems in their work. Most employees would choose to know if their supervisor is upset about something they are doing so that they can do something to correct the problem.

Assertive supervisors realize that constructive feedback benefits themselves as well as the employees. Addressing mistakes or below-standard work in a nonjudgmental, problem-solving manner benefits employees by giving them the opportunity to do something about the problems. Supervisors benefit because errors and low performance are kept at a minimum. They feel more in control of their job and, thus, more confident.

One business expert said, "I have yet to find the person, however exalted his or her position, who did not do better work and put forth greater effort under a spirit of approval than under a spirit of criticism." It is the privilege of supervisors to criticize the work of their staff. Yet good leaders will criticize in constructive, helpful ways. They know that the power to criticize is a tremendous responsibility; they handle it gently. Criticism can easily slip over into petty fault finding, which the employee will quite rightly resent. Supervisors who find fault with everything will hardly inspire people to do their best.

FACTORS THAT HINDER CONSTRUCTIVE FEEDBACK

The "I-Can't" Attitude

Passive supervisors accept the "I-can't" beliefs because they attach little importance to what is occurring and accept problems with resignation. The I-can't attitude is most often manifested in the following four ways:

1. *Disregarding the problem.* This is done by taking little account of the situation and not caring about oneself or others. The I-can't supervisor turns the other way, believing that the problem will disappear. You might hear him or her say, "It really doesn't make any difference" (when it does) or "It will blow away if I just wait long enough" (when it won't).

   CASE   Mark, a supervisor on an assembly line, is often unsure about the instructions he gives his workers but does not take the time to make sure those instructions are correct. He sometimes watches an assembler do a task incorrectly and then does nothing about it, saying to himself, "It's no big deal; anyway, Joseph would get upset if I said anything."

2. *Denying the significance of the problem.* This is done when a supervi-

sor who has a project due says, "They won't miss it; they probably wouldn't read it anyway." The I-can't supervisor might try to justify inaction by denying that there is a problem in the first place. He or she might say, "You take it too seriously; it really isn't a problem. It's all in your head."

3. *Denying the solvability of the problem.* The I-can't supervisor makes statements like, "There's no answer," "It's just too big," or "There's nothing that can be done about it." The result is a refusal to look at alternatives, to find new ways of approaching problems, to learn new skills, to acquire new knowledge, or to change old strategies that no longer work.

4. *Disregarding oneself.* The person with an I-can't attitude often denies his or her own capacity to solve a problem. This I-can't supervisor makes statements such as "I just can't solve these kinds of problems, they are too complex" or "I can't handle difficult people because the situation will get worse" or "I can't confront late employees because they will get angry." The result is that problems go unresolved, difficult situations get worse, and staff morale decreases.

Most people occasionally behave from these self-defeating beliefs. However, when supervisors get caught up in them consistently, they experience serious problems that can result in crises. The key is to be aware of when it happens so that you can stop yourself and move into the assertive mode. Ask yourself, "What would be the most useful thing for me to do about the problem? What resources do I have at my disposal?" Then develop an action plan and carry it out.

The "You-Should" Attitude

Supervisors with the "you-should" attitude often use the aggressive supervisory style. The "you-should" attitude perpetuates the distancing/resisting environment you learned about in Chapter 5 (see pages 98–99). You-should supervisors do this in several ways: by setting unrealistic standards, by using an aggressive behavioral style and a biased listening style, and by communicating in a hostile way.

Unrealistic Standards

Supervisors who set unrealistic standards for their employees are often caught up in the belief that people "should be perfect" and that if they aren't, "there's something wrong with them."

CASE   Craig, a supervisor for a large accounting firm, prides himself on his "high standards." However, the twelve people he supervises feel they can never do anything right. They say, "There's just no pleasing Craig!" No matter what they hand in to Craig, he finds something wrong with it. Because of his unrealistic demands, Craig's negative feedback far outweighs his positive comments. Instead of improving, employee performance is getting worse.

It is important for supervisors to have high expectations of their employees. You will find some guidance in setting performance standards later in this chapter.

Judgmental Attitudes

A major part of the you-should attitude is judging others from a strict judgmental framework of right-wrong, bad-good. This rigidity interferes with the supervisor's ability to objectively observe what the employee is doing. Most employees resent being judged and respond negatively.

The key is to be aware of the difference between how you behave when you can "step back" and witness events nonemotionally versus how you behave when you quickly judge emotionally from a strict, judgmental framework.

Judgmental behavior often starts with biases. This results in name calling, putdowns, and the use of "red flag" words. Biases can result in a supervisor's prejudging as unimportant what an employee is going to say or in distorting what the employee has said.

"Red flag" words are words or statements to which people are sensitive—they are words to which a stigma is attached, such as the following:

lack	stupid	must
careless	slow poke	always
weakness	never	lazy
should	have to	all the time
stupid	rude	thoughtless

You fail to understand.	Do I have to show you again?
You are confused.	Don't you know what you're doing?
I told you so.	Why can't you do anything right?

Putting labels on people is another way of judging. Labeling employees is a way of treating them as nonpersons; it prevents you from understanding them more fully. Labels make it appear that you know your employees; you may convince yourself you do. However, your knowledge stopped at the superficial. Labels replace human beings as people; they become mere "types" in your eyes.

Still another dimension of judging is the use of putdowns. You may get caught using putdowns when you are unsure of yourself or have a need to stay one-up on the other person. It's important to stop using putdowns altogether. When you are about to use a putdown, ask yourself this question: "Is my need to put this person down a function of my confidence, self-esteem, and self-assurance, or a sign of self-doubt and a lack of self-assurance?"

Misplaced humor is another form of judging. When people believe that others have little value, they will treat them in negative ways. Misuse of humor is one of them. A sense of humor is an essential characteristic of success. However, when it is used at the expense of another, its value has been lost. Here is an example:

EMPLOYEE: "Clayton, how would you have handled this situation?"
SUPERVISOR: "Under an assumed name!"

This type of retort doesn't help the employee handle the problem more effectively or enhance his or her self-esteem.

APPROACHES THAT WILL ASSIST YOU IN GIVING CONSTRUCTIVE FEEDBACK

Now that you have had an opportunity to examine the various factors that interfere with giving constructive feedback, take a look at some learning tools to handle this critical supervisory function. Supervisors who build on people's strengths, rather than harping too much on what is being done incorrectly, usually reap the fruit of their positive attitude. They consistently find ways to improve the performance of those they supervise.

Realistic Performance Standards

A *standard* is an established measure for comparison and evaluation. It is the yardstick against which you measure the quantity, quality, and manner of an employee's performance. It is best to base your criticism of your employees on *realistic* performance standards. The following outline of the main types of standards will assist you in evaluating the standards you have developed or in establishing new ones.

- *Quantity,* expressed by

   Amount: a definite number, a range, a portion or "fair share" of total work load

   Time limit: within what time; by deadline; by priority order; by a set time to avoid undesirable results

   Note: It is almost always necessary to show both *amount* and *time limit.*

- *Quality,* expressed by

   Appearance of finished product

   Results achieved

   Accuracy (degree of freedom from error)

- *Manner of Performance,* including

   Methods of work procedures

   Knowledge required (beyond basic entrance requirements)

   Personal characteristics of employee

Some Tests of a Fair Performance Standard

It is important that the standard be set at the level that will get the job done satisfactorily. The standard is not necessarily perfection; it's best that it not be so high that no one can be rated "outstanding" nor so low that everyone can be rated "outstanding."

The standard is based on the job requirements, not on performance of present employees; it is best that the standard be what could be expected of any basically qualified person assigned to the job.

The standard has preferably been developed in consultation with the employee.

The standard is current.

The standard has requirements that the supervisor can check on fairly and accurately.

Focus on Understanding and Reaching Agreement

Rarely can a supervisor *coerce* a worker into putting forth better work. Coercion can sometimes produce short-term results, but what usually accompanies the results is fear, resentment, or sabotage. The significant factor in effectively applying constructive feedback is being skilled in communication techniques that can lead to understanding, agreement, and harmony, rather than in the judgmental approach that leads to misunderstanding, disagreement, and crises. Drawing out the other person to express his or her viewpoint will create the environment needed to direct dialogue toward an agreement acceptable to all parties.

One way to do this is to approach the critical issue from a coaching stance. In other words, turn criticism into a coaching session. Examine how you can use what was done incorrectly to coach the employee to do it correctly the next time around.

Open-Ended and Loaded Questions

An ingredient to assist you in assuming a coaching stance is the use of open-ended questions—door openers. Open-ended questions are those that cannot be answered with just yes or no or some other simple answer, like a number. They promote a noncoercive invitation to employees to express their opinions and feelings truthfully, regardless of whether they are favorable or unfavorable to your point of view. The following are examples of open-ended questions:

- What are your ideas about . . . ?
- How could you have . . . ?
- What do you feel about . . . ?
- What do you think of . . . ?

Open-ended questions have several benefits:

- They show your interest in the employee.
- They help the employee feel more comfortable and secure because he or she isn't being grilled but given an opportunity to be heard.
- They draw the employee out, letting you hear more about what is on the employee's mind.
- They help you focus on performance or the issue, thus helping you not to get caught up on moral judgments or personalities.

Loaded questions, on the other hand, set a trap or induce the employee to respond in a predetermined direction. When this happens, employees have a strong tendency to justify and defend their actions. Feeling they are being pushed into a direction that isn't their choice, they perceive the supervisor as an opponent to resist rather than an ally with whom to cooperate. Discussion is cut off, freedom of response is curtailed, and openness is reduced.

EXERCISE 7.1	## Open-Ended and Loaded Questions

The following questions will test your ability to identify the difference between open-ended and loaded questions. Put a circle around the number of each open-ended question.

1. Would you like more responsibility?

2. Don't you think you would enjoy a new assignment?

3. What has been causing your lateness?

4. What kind of actions could you take to increase the number of sales calls you make per day?

5. Don't you think you should try to be on time?

6. How many calls a day do you feel you need to make to reach your sales quota?

7. How would you feel about having increased responsibility?

8. Tell me more about how you see your present assignment and what you want in the future.

9. Why don't you make as many sales calls as our more successful sales representatives?

10. If going over budget bothers you, as you say it does, why have you done it so often?

11. What concerns you about meeting the budget?

Answers:

Open-ended questions: 3, 4, 6, 7, 8, and 11.
Loaded questions: 1, 2, 5, 9, and 10.

1. Would you like more responsibility? (Yes/No. This cuts off discussion.)

2. Don't you think you would enjoy a new assignment? (Directing question. It cuts down freedom of response.)

5. Don't you think you should try to be on time? (Setting a trap! Will probably lead to defensiveness.)

9. Why don't you make as many sales calls as our more successful sales representatives? (Leading question. Will probably lead to defensiveness.)

10. If going over budget bothers you, as you say it does, why have you done it so often? (Cross-examination, directive question. Reduces openness and perpetuates defensiveness.)

It's important to be aware that open questions, like any other effective techniques, can be misused. Sometimes a supervisor who is eager to use a technique overuses it. The following is an example:

SUPERVISOR: "You look sad, John. Feel like talking?"
JOHN: "Not really."
SUPERVISOR: "I can tell you are troubled. You know you can talk to me."
JOHN: "I don't feel like it right now."
SUPERVISOR: "You really ought to get it off your chest, you know."
JOHN: "Yeah, I know. Later, maybe."
SUPERVISOR: "But the time to talk is when you are feeling things. Come on, John . . ."

The assertive supervisor respects the privacy of the employee and honors the employee's right to talk or to remain silent when approached. The assertive supervisor uses empathetic listening and open-ended questions to invite conversation, not to compel the employee to talk.

Other Styles of Questioning

There are various types of questions you can use to help you give constructive feedback. Having a variety of questioning styles at your disposal will assist you in being more comfortable in approaching unpleasant situations.

STYLES OF QUESTIONING		
Style	**Purpose**	**Examples**
Factual	• To acquire information • To open discussion	• *Who, what, how, where,* and *when* questions

STYLES OF QUESTIONING

Style	Purpose	Examples
Searching	• To get reasons and explanations; to expand discussion • To develop additional information	• "In what way would this help solve the problem?" • "What other aspects of this could be considered?" • "How would this be done?"
Declaring	• To challenge old ideas • To develop new ideas • To examine reasoning and proof	• "How do you know that would work?" • "What evidence do you have?" • "Why do you think so?"
Input	• To introduce a new idea • To advance a suggestion of your own	• "Could we consider this as a possible solution?" • "Would this be a feasible alternative?"
Supposition	• To develop a new idea • To suggest another, perhaps unpopular, opinion to change the course of discussion	• "What would happen if we did it this way?" • "Another company does this—would this be feasible here?" • "What do they do in other companies that could work here?"
Option	• To make decisions between alternatives • To get agreement	• "Which of these solutions is best—A or B?" • "Is A our choice in preference to B?"
Collaborative	• To get agreement • To pave the way for action	• "Can we conclude that this is the next step?" • "Is there general agreement on this plan?"

These kinds of questions will help you effectively apply constructive feedback while moving conflict situations through to agreement and resolution.

Leveling Method

Another approach that will aid you in applying constructive feedback is the leveling method. This method focuses on treating the employee as an equal. The intention is to create a cooperative environment that will enhance agreement and problem solving. The following guidelines will help you apply the leveling method.

1. Be a witness rather than a judge. Focus on what would be useful to do—not on blaming.

2. Get the facts. Weigh all the circumstances.

3. Provide feedback face to face, in private.

4. Discuss any problem while the incident is fresh in your mind, before your memory is able to garble the events. The longer you wait, the more your recollection of events will differ from what actually happened. Moreover, if you wait too long, you will lose the indignant feeling that motivates assertive acts. So assert yourself as soon as you can.

5. Stay with the immediate problem; don't bring up past problems regarding other issues.

6. Don't begin by saying how terrible the problem is: "There's something terrible happening here. It's really getting me mad. What I mean is . . ." Such a preface makes the other person defensive. If you need a preface, just say, "I'd like to speak to you about something I've noticed."

7. Comment on what a person does, not on what you imagine that person is.

8. Be specific; avoid generalizations: "You have been absent three Fridays"; "You have missed two deadlines."

9. Be objective: "Your manner resulted in two customers complaining about the way you treated them," not "You've been extremely rude."

10. Use words that relate to specific actions rather than words that label characteristics: "*He was silent* through the whole meeting" not "*He sulked and pouted* through the whole meeting."

11. Assume a leveling, nonverbal posture. This involves looking straight at the listener, keeping eye contact 60 percent of the time, squaring the head and face so you achieve a level-headed posture, and relaxing the body.

12. Listen at level 1. Be attentive; use acknowledging words: "I see," "Gee," "Hmm," "Uh-huh." People prefer vocal stroking to silence.

13. Use positive movement by leaning forward, being attentive, nodding your head in agreement, and, when appropriate, touching the speaker's arm.

14. Smile, look interested, and sincerely use other positive facial expressions. People quickly recognize a false front.

15. Apply the empathetic listening approach. Summarize and clarify to avoid misunderstandings.

The "I-Rational" Approach*

An essential ingredient of constructive feedback is the "I-rational" approach. It will assist in reducing resistance, allow you to make constructive feedback when it is needed, and increase the possibility of reaching agreement on unpleasant issues.

Supervisors who have not learned this approach often criticize by using the "you-blaming" approach. The problem with the you-blaming approach is that it builds resistance, turns people off, and leads to disagreement and misunderstanding. The following summary of both approaches will help you understand how they are different.

I-Rational Approach	You-Blaming Approach
Leads to a win/win resolution, both people feeling the solution meets needs.	Leads to a win/lose resolution, one person feeling victorious, the other defeated.
Plan of action is developed to achieve the best outcome.	Plan of action usually not developed.
Discloses something one person is unhappy about in the hopes of modifying other's and own behavior by problem solving.	Discloses something one person is unhappy about to let the other know he or she *should* or *ought* to change.
Based on an OK/OK frame of reference.	Based on an OK/not-OK frame of reference.

*From *Listening: The Forgotten Skill*, by Madelyn Burley-Allen (New York: John Wiley & Sons, 1982).

I-Rational Approach	You-Blaming Approach
Confrontation occurs in a rational, objective, and not overly emotional way. Is aware of the impact nonverbal has on others; is conscious of gestures, posture, facial expression, tone of voice.	Confrontation occurs in a way that is overly emotional, subjective, irrational. Does not take into account the importance of the nonverbal aspects of the communication process.
Messages are stated in a nonblaming, noncritical manner; no putdowns.	Messages are stated in a blaming, critical, judgmental manner, namecalling, stereotyping, attacking, threatening.
Each person takes responsibility for own feelings: "I feel upset . . ."	Each person puts the responsibility for own feelings on the other person: "You make me upset . . ."
Each person observes and states specifically the behavior that is troubling him or her.	Each person labels behaviors as good or bad, right or wrong.
Avoidance of words that tend to push "hot buttons."	Use of words that tend to push "hot buttons," such as *you should, you ought to, you must, never, always, all the time, rude, stupid,* and *lazy.*

The following examples of the two approaches will give you an idea of how they are different, plus provide you with guidelines for developing your own.

I-Rational Approach	You-Blaming Approach
"When you talk on the phone instead of working on my report, I feel concerned that my report will not be completed by the due date."	"You're always talking on the phone! You should stop because you don't get your work done."
"When you talk to others about nonbusiness affairs away from your work area, I feel concerned about your work and the effect on others because a team spirit is disrupted."	"You're never in your work area and always disrupting other people."

I-Rational Approach	You-Blaming Approach
"I'm very concerned that you took a 30-minute break this morning. It delays break time for others and means others have to cover your desk as well as their own."	"You make me angry when you always take longer breaks than you should."
"When you involve yourself in situations that don't concern you, I feel frustrated because this causes resentment among your co-workers that results in lower productivity."	"You're always interfering in situations that aren't your business and making other people angry."

You may find developing and expressing I-rational statements somewhat difficult. Don't feel alone! Many people have some difficulty with it. The reason for the difficulty is most likely you weren't trained to express yourself nonjudgmentally, so the hardest thing you will experience is staying out of judgment. You will find it easier to express an I-rational statement after you work with them for a while. It helps to say the I-rational statement either out loud or quietly to yourself to hear how it sounds.

The statement has three components to it: nonjudgmental description of the behavior, your feelings, and the results/impact of the behavior. Your statements don't always have to follow this format. There will be times, because of the situation and/or personality of the person with whom you are dealing, when you may want to state your feelings first, then describe the person's behavior, and follow that by the results/impact. Sometimes you may want to state the results/impact first, then describe the behavior, and finally your feelings.

The order you choose will be determined by the situation, the personality of the other person, and your own personality. In addition, you don't always need to use all three components. If you have difficulty expressing your feelings or the person with whom you are communicating has difficulty dealing with feelings, drop the feeling part of the statement. Describe their behavior nonjudgmentally and state the results/impact. The important ingredient is staying out of judgment.

Poor Example: "I'm concerned when you always miss deadlines because we never get our projects done on time."

Correct Example: "I'm concerned that you missed the deadline on the Johnson report yesterday because it reduces our creditability with management."

If you used the poor example, you could very likely perpetuate a "Yes, but . . ." reaction: "Yes, but I don't always miss deadlines" or "Yes, but I didn't miss a deadline last year!" Once that happens you could lose control of the situation.

It is essential that the I-rational statement be directed at the *other* person's needs. I-rational statements won't work if your needs and the other person's needs don't match. More than likely, you are stating your I-rational statement because you want the other person to change, to do something different, or to improve. People will respond to your I-rational statement if the results/impact is meaningful to them. Your job is to persuade them by directing the statement to what interests them, what they value, or what they care about. Ask yourself what results/impact does the other person value—saving time, increasing productivity, morale, team building, image, creditability, improvement, money, promotion, relationships, accuracy, and so on.

You might have experienced confronting someone about an issue and gotten the reaction, "It's your problem, not mine" or something like that. This is an example of missing the mark. This kind of reaction indicates that the person didn't have the same values or interests as you. People generally are persuaded to change or improve if there is something in it for them. The only way you can get someone to change or improve if they *don't* want to is through punishment, fear, threats, or coercion. This type of behavior fits the aggressive style. An assertive supervisor won't use these methods as they most certainly will lower self-esteem and influence the other to dig in and to resent or rebel.

Remember that the other person has choice as to how he or she respond to your I-rational statement. Allowing them freedom of choice will help you get what you want. When people feel that they are being told they "should" or "must" or "ought to," their internal "rebel kid" will resent and rebel. Most people want to be liked and will cooperate if there is something in your statement about which they care.

An effective statement is one of the best tools to assist you in being assertive and having a positive influence on others. This is because you are expressing to them from the OK–OK attitude and at level 1. It is important to be prepared for what the other will say in response to your statement. Remember to be an empathetic listener, summarize or paraphrase what was said, ask clarifying questions—who, what, when, and how (Chapter 5, pages 119–120)—explore alternatives, develop a plan, and follow up. This procedure will help you and the other person communicate in a dialogue fashion that will move the interaction to a positive solution.

EXERCISE 7.2   **Employee Performance Analysis***

To practice this I-rational approach, complete the following analysis.

1. Take a moment to think about those you supervise. Choose one employee to whom you want to give constructive feedback. What is this employee's name?

2. What is the behavior that you want the employee to correct or improve?

3. How is the employee performing now?

4. What do you want him or her to do?

5. Type of performance problem (check one).
   _____ Not done often enough
   _____ Not done correctly
   _____ Both of the above
   _____ Other _____

6. Review the list below and check each factor that influences this person's performance.
   _____ Co-workers support or at least do not interfere with desirable performance.
   _____ Employee gets input that is adequate to perform as desired.
   _____ Physical environment is adequate for desired performance.
   _____ Performance requires only skills and knowledge that employee already has or could acquire with proper feedback.
   _____ Consequences of performance are appropriate.
   _____ Other _____

7. Check each statement that represents a probable deficiency in the way feedback is currently provided.
   _____ Not given at all
   _____ Comes too late to be meaningful
   _____ Comes too soon to be useful
   _____ Given *only* when something is wrong
   _____ Given in a you-blaming way

*Adapted from Operants, Inc., San Rafael, CA, 94903

_____ Focuses on personality rather than performance
_____ Not given in sufficient detail
_____ Other _____

8. *I-Rational Guidelines*

Now that you have specifically examined the behavior in question, complete an I-rational description in the following table. Note the person's behavior in the first column, your feelings in the second column, and the results of his or her behavior in the third column.

Nonjudgmental Description of the Behavior	My Feelings	Results/Impact

9. *Putting It Together*

Using the information you noted in Exercise 8, write a concise, descriptive I-rational statement.

"When you _____,
(nonjudgmental description of other's behavior)

I feel _____
(feelings)

because _____

_____
(results/impact)

10. *Measurement*

Describe the means of measuring performance. How will you know when you have succeeded?

EXERCISE 7.3	**Practice Session—I-Rational Statements**

As additional practice, change the following you-blaming statements into I-rational statements.

1. Someone in the office has parked in your reserved space. You-blaming statement: "You're not being considerate of me. You know that is my space, not yours. Why don't you park in your own space as you're supposed to?"

   I-rational statement:

2. An employee left early yesterday without letting you know. You-blaming statement: "You're always leaving early without letting me know. Your inconsiderate behavior has caused a lot of problems."

   I-rational statement:

3. June, a supervisor from another department, doesn't return your phone calls. You-blaming statement: "If you weren't so disorganized, you'd see my phone messages on your desk. It's really annoying to have to call you three or four times to get information I need from you."

   I-rational statement:

Possible Answers:

Compare your I-rational statements with the following. If your statements differ, make sure that your statements follow the ground rules for the I-rational approach as noted on page 159.

1. "When I go to park in my reserve parking space and find your car parked there, I get frustrated because I'm certain you know it's my space. What happened?"

2. "I am puzzled that you didn't let me know that you were planning to leave early. Please clarify what happened."

3. "June, when you don't return my phone calls, I get concerned because it delays getting my work completed on time."

Conducting the Performance Interview

The leveling guidelines and the I-rational approach should assist you in providing constructive feedback pertaining to a performance issue. The following guidelines go into specifics about the exact steps to follow.

Guidelines

I. Conducting the interview by using the leveling approach.

  A. Set the stage.
    1. Be informal and establish a friendly atmosphere.
    2. Explain the purpose by making your I-rational statements.
    3. Make it clear that the discussion is a two-way conversation, a mutual problem-solving and goal-setting exchange.

  B. Discuss format.
    1. Follow the leveling approach on page 158.
    2. Cite specific examples.
    3. Encourage employee to discuss how he or she appraises his or her own performance.
      a. Use open-ended questions.
      b. Ask clarifying questions.
      c. Be an empathetic listener.
    4. Summarize and clarify employee's remarks to help him or her see the logic of their thoughts and to assist him to reach understanding of their problems.
    5. Mutually discuss suggestions for eliminating the problem.
      a. Encourage the employee to set self-targets.
      b. Assist him or her in achieving these targets.
    6. Reach agreement on the development of the plans to reach the targets. Plans should spell out what the two of you are going to do and how success will be measured.

  C. Ending the discussion.
    1. Summarize what has been discussed.
      a. Make it positive.
      b. Show enthusiasm for the plans made.
    2. Give employee an opportunity to make any additional suggestions.
    3. Close discussion on a friendly, harmonious note.

II. Postinterview Activity

    A. Make a record of:
       1. Items on which you agreed and disagreed.
       2. Areas in which employee is sensitive.
       3. Any new background information.
       4. Items for future review.
       5. Plans you and employee have made (with a copy to the employee).
       6. Points requiring follow-up.
       7. Commitments you have made for action on your part.
    B. Evaluate how you handled the discussion.
       1. What did you do well?
       2. On what could you improve?
       3. What would you do differently?
       4. What did you learn about the employee?
       5. What did you learn about your job?
    C. Follow up; assist the employee to adjust to the constructive changes upon which you agreed.

SUMMARY

In this chapter, you learned how certain factors hinder constructive feedback, such as self-limiting and rigid beliefs, passive behavior, unrealistic standards, and judgmental attitudes. You learned techniques to assist in applying constructive feedback. Emphasis was put on the understanding and agreement-reaching approach, including the use of open-ended questions, various styles of questioning, leveling, and the I-rational approach.

A format for conducting a performance interview incorporating the techniques covered in the chapter was provided. This format will aid you in handling performance problems with more confidence.

8 Saying No

The measure of success is not whether you have a tough problem to deal with, but whether it's the same problem you had last year.

John Foster Dulles

The biggest mistake you can make is to believe that you are working for someone else.

Unknown

As a supervisor, you play a unique role in your organization because you exist between the workers and the rest of the superstructure of management. The position of the supervisor is most significant. Regardless of how good the plans of higher management are in theory, they are worthless in practice unless your supervisory skills are such that you can carry them out effectively. A critical skill necessary for this effectiveness is the ability to say no, the fifth building block of managing assertivity.

Most supervisors find that *no* is one of the hardest words for them to say face-to-face. Of course, these supervisors can say no sometimes, to some people; the difficulty lies in being able to say no to anyone and in any situation. To help you discover the situations that prevent you from saying no, complete the following assessment exercise.

EXERCISE 8.1 **Assessing Your Ability to Say No**

To identify the problem areas you might have in regard to saying no, complete this assessment. On the line next to each statement, write the number that best indicates how that statement applies to you.

0 Not true
1 Somewhat true
2 Largely true
3 True

_____ 1. I find it easy to say no to my boss when he or she requests work I don't have time to complete.

_____ 2. I can say no when a peer asks me to help get a project out if it would result in my getting behind schedule.

_____ 3. I can say I don't agree when I am offered an alternative that I don't go along with.

_____ 4. I can say no when an employee pushes unrealistic demands on me.

_____ 5. I am able to say no to my manager when I am asked to employ new methods that will affect morale.

_____ 6. I can say no to establish my limits with my boss.

_____ 7. I can say no to establish my limits with my employees.

_____ 8. I am able to say no to someone who is asking for information I am not allowed to give out.

_____ 9. I can say no persistently, as often as necessary; when a person is demanding of me something that I definitely cannot give.

_____10. I can say no even when someone is trying to manipulate me by sulking, crying, or getting angry.

_____11. I can say no without feeling guilty.

_____12. I can say no without feeling fearful.

Discussion of Exercise 8.1

1. Review your assessment. Choose those behavioral statements that you feel you like or are able to handle effectively. Copy those statements here.

2. Choose those behavioral statements that you want to modify or improve. Copy them here.

3. Examine those behaviors you want to improve by means of the A→B→C→D belief model. Use the first behavior you listed.

A = Event: What kinds of situations and people are involved when you aren't able to say no? Note the person's name and describe the situation.

B = Thought Process: What do you say internally that causes you to behave the way you do? Describe your internal dialogue.

C = OK Attitude: Identify it.

D = Outcome: Behavior/Feeling: Describe how you behave and feel as a result of your thought process.

It is hoped that this exercise helped you pinpoint the specific people and situations on the job that are giving you trouble and gave you a method to overcome your self-defeating behavior.

SAYING NO AND THE THREE SUPERVISORY STYLES

How would supervisors with the passive, aggressive, and assertive supervisory styles handle saying no?

The Passive Supervisor

Supervisors behaving in this style allow themselves to be manipulated by guilt, anger, threats, pleas for help, and tears. Their strongest emotions are fear, which stops them from saying no, and guilt, which they feel when they do say no. The beliefs they have about saying no include, "I can't . . .," "I shouldn't . . .," "I'll never be able to say no," and "I wish I could, but I can't." The beliefs of passive supervisors result in their having a self-concept of being unable to say no, picturing mentally this inability and failure. These beliefs result in their operating most often from the I'm-not-OK—you're-OK attitude.

Passive supervisors often will not delegate work for fear the employee won't like it. They won't express their ideas or opinions for fear others won't like them or will say no to them. Not saying no to peers and others in management positions results in their being overburdened with tasks that aren't really their responsibility. This, in turn, results in their not having enough time to complete their own tasks satisfactorily.

CASE   Angie is a supervisor responsible for a pool of six secretaries in a large manufacturing plant. The fourteen people to whom she and her workers are responsible have high work demands. Joseph, a manager in another department, often asks Angie to "squeeze in" short typing jobs for him. His manipulation takes the form of pleas mixed with flattery: "You know that your girls are much more accurate than the secretaries in our department, and it won't take very long this once. If I don't get this done right now, I'll be in deep trouble."

Unless Angie can say no, her workers will be overburdened with unnecessary work and feelings of resentment toward her.

The inability of passive supervisors to say no has grave effects when a boss asks them to complete a task by an unrealistic deadline. When they don't say no, they take on tasks that are impossible to complete in the designated time frame. This leads to failure to meet the required deadline, workers feeling bad, and a boss who is unsatisfied with the supervisor's performance. The passive style results in an overextension of oneself and one's employees that promotes stress, poor time management, and an image as a pushover.

Some passive supervisors use an indirect no as a way out of their self-imposed bind.

CASE   When an unrealistic demand is made of Howard, he responds, "I'll try to get it done." His promise to "try" is really a no, since he knows he won't be able to get it done. Because he is fearful of saying no, he says "I'll try" instead.

Another form of an indirect no Howard uses is the hidden aggressive behavior mode. If you ask him to do something he doesn't have time to do, instead of assertively saying no, Howard says yes, feeling that you would think less of him for not being able to do it. He may also feel you are making demands of him, blame and resent you for his negative feelings, and end up making you not-OK and feeling not-OK about himself. Howard's saying yes when he wants to say no prevents the two of you from working out the problem to your mutual satisfaction.

The Aggressive Supervisor

Whereas passive supervisors have difficulty saying no, the aggressive supervisor has no qualms about it. The aggressive supervisor says no without hesitation and arbitrarily, with little thought about how important it might be to the other person to know the reasons for the no. Thus, employees perceive the aggressive supervisor's no as having no real cause and, thus, respond with defensiveness and resistance.

CASE Walter's favorite OK attitude is I'm OK–you're not OK. His attitude is that his rights are more important than the rights of others. When Walter says no, there is no room for working out possible alternatives. His belief system consists of "shoulds," "have tos," and "musts" in excess, leaving little choice of actions to others. He expresses his ideas and opinions with the attitude, "If they don't like it, that's their problem." This attitude comes across as intimidating and perpetuates resistance, hidden aggression, hostility, and uncooperativeness in those with whom he deals. Walter doesn't understand why his employees don't work as hard as he does or perform at maximum level, or why people ask to be transferred from his department.

Employees who are not allowed to express themselves or to work out problems to mutual agreement feel disempowered and often respond by doing only as much as they must to get by. When supervisors use no to excess, it often produces a stressful environment, resulting in reduced creativity, lack of team work, absenteeism, turnover, and physical illnesses.

The Assertive Supervisor

Assertive supervisors have learned that demands are a part of the job of a supervisor. Thus, they have learned how important it is to deal with saying no in an assertive manner. They realize that, led by their own self-interest, others may take advantage of people who cannot say no. These supervisors know that it is better not to depend on others to look out for one's own best interests; that is one's own responsibility.

Assertive supervisors have jumped the hurdle of being afraid that others will think them uncooperative. They have found it is better to be truthful about their feelings and what they can do than to be dishonest and make promises they can't fulfill. They use various methods to work out alternative options.

The assertive approach includes being aware of the importance of nonverbal communication and realizing how much can be expressed without saying a word. Because saying no is a way to set limits, assertive supervisors think before they say it, have a reason, and know what they expect.

WHEN TO SAY NO

Being able to say no can earn respect from others and increase your self-respect. This ability can also help you overcome feelings of powerlessness. Many negative repercussions can be avoided if the refusal is done assertively. The focus is on *how* you say no rather than the fact that you have said it. Your attitude plays a major part in your ability to successfully say no with a positive outcome. The following guidelines will assist you in your endeavor.

1. Ask yourself:

- Do I *want* to do this, or am I trying to please someone else?

- What will I receive for my participation?

- If I agree to do this, will it continue to be rewarding, or will it become oppressive?

2. Think it over:

- Give yourself time to evaluate the request. Assess whether the request is reasonable or unreasonable. It's not necessary to commit yourself to something as soon as you are asked to do it.

- You might say, "Let me think it over and get back to you." Then, get back to them.

3. Clues that the request may be unreasonable:

- Do you find yourself hesitating or hedging?

- Do you feel cornered or trapped?

- Do you feel a tightness somewhere in your body?

- Do you feel a nervous reaction?

4. If needed, ask for more information or clarification.

5. Hold an attitude that the situation can be resolved from a win-win framework. Agree on something favorable to all parties.

6. Allow for discussion of ideas and differences of opinions.

7. Focus on the problem, not on personalities. Move toward negotiating on points of differences. Don't overcommit yourself.

Expressing Your No

Once you understand the request and decide you want to say no, choose the kind of no that best suits the person and situation. Here are some general rules to follow.

1. Say no, firmly and calmly, without saying, "I'm sorry," which weakens your stand.

2. Say no, followed by a straightforward explanation of what you are feeling or what you are willing to do, such as: "I'm uncomfortable doing that," "I'm not willing to do that," "I don't want to do that," "I don't like to do that."

3. Say no, and then give a choice or alternative, such as: "Not now; however, I will when I get this done, which could be in an hour," or "I don't have time today, but I could help out the first thing tomorrow morning."

4. Say no, then clarify your reasons. This does not include long-winded statements filled with excuses, justifications, and rationalizations. It's enough that you do not want to say yes. Your clarification is given to provide the receiver more information so that he or she can better understand your position.

5. Use your natural no. You may have developed your own style of saying no based on your past experience and personality. If so, use it.

6. Make an empathetic listening statement, then say no. You may paraphrase the content and feeling of the request, then state your no; for example: "I can see that it is important to you that one of my secretaries get your report done. I'd like to have someone do it, but my staff is already overburdened with high priority tasks to be completed by the end of the day."

7. Say yes, then give your reasons for *not* doing it or your alternative solution. This approach is very interesting. You may want to use it in

situations when you are willing to meet the request, but *not* at the time or in the way the other person wants it; for example: "Yes, I would be willing to help you out, but I won't have time until tomorrow afternoon," "Yes, I could have part of your report typed, but not all forty pages," "Yes, I'd be willing to go along with your second alternative, but not the third one you suggested."

8. *The Persistent Response** This method of saying no entails using a one-sentence refusal statement and persistently repeating it as often as necessary, no matter what the person says. This technique is useful when dealing with very aggressive or manipulative people who "won't take no for an answer." It is especially useful to assist you in moving from the passive mode to the assertive mode because it gives you a specific format to follow. It is also useful for moving yourself away from the extreme aggressive end of the continuum, if you are apt to lose control and become verbally abusive. The persistent response can be effective in maintaining your refusal while continuing to be in charge of your emotions.

Because the persistent-response way of saying no is unusual and a bit complex, the following detailed guidelines for applying it are provided for you.

Persistent-Response Guidelines

1. Select a concise, one-sentence statement and repeat it, no matter what the other person says or does; for example: "I understand how you feel, but I'm not willing . . ."; I'm not interested . . ."; "I don't want to . . ."; "I'm uncomfortable doing that, so I don't want to . . ."; "You might be right, but I'm not interested."

2. After each statement by the other person, say your persistent response sentence. It's important that you don't get sidetracked by responding to any issue the other person brings up.

3. Say your statement firmly, calmly, and as unemotionally as possible.

4. Be aware of your nonverbal behavior, making sure you don't come across passively or aggressively. Use plenty of silence to your advantage. Your silence will project the message that the other's statements and manipulation are futile.

*Adapted from *When I Say No, I Feel Guilty*, by Dr. Manuel Smith (New York: Dial Press, 1975).

5. Be persistent. Simply state your response one more time than the other person makes his or her request, question, or statement. If the other person makes six statements, you make seven. If the other person makes three statements, you make four. Most often, the other person will feel ill at ease and stop after three or four statements. Other times, your response will move the other person to offer options with which you *are* willing to go along.

The following two dialogues are examples of how this approach could be used:

Dialogue 1: Between a salesperson and Mary, the purchasing supervisor of a large electronics company, who is in charge of purchasing office equipment for her company.

SALESPERSON: "Good morning! I was told by your secretary that you are interested in replacing a number of office chairs and desks in your technical department."

MARY: "Yes, I am, but I have already decided on the company I'm going to buy them from."

SALESPERSON: "You should reconsider. I'm sure we can give you a better deal."

MARY: "That might be true, but the decision has already been made and the order placed."

SALESPERSON: "Don't you want to save money for your company?"

MARY: "You're right, I do, but the decision has already been made."

SALESPERSON: "What kind of purchasing supervisor are you? Don't you want to save money?"

MARY: "The decision has already been made."

SALESPERSON: "Is your manager in? I'm sure he would be interested in saving some money."

MARY: "I understand you want to sell your furniture, but the decision has already been made."

SALESPERSON: "Don't you want to do the best for your company?"

MARY: "You're right, I do, but the decision has already been made."

SALESPERSON: "You won't give an inch, will you?"

MARY: "You're right, I won't."

SALESPERSON: "Well, here's my card. When you're buying furniture in the future, call me."

MARY: "Thank you, I might do that."

Dialogue 2: Between Jim and his manager, Kent. It is Wednesday afternoon, and Kent is asking Jim to complete a project by Friday. Jim knows from past experience that this type of project takes a week to ten days to complete.

KENT: "Jim, I need this project done by Friday and no later."

JIM: "I won't be able to get it done in that time—it takes a week to ten days to complete that kind of project."

KENT: "I don't care how long it took in the past; I want it done by Friday."

JIM: "Kent, I can understand your wanting to get this out by Friday, but it's impossible because of the number of hours it takes to get it done. It can be completed by Wednesday afternoon if I put two extra people on it."

KENT: "You don't realize how important it is to get this done by Friday. It must be done by then!"

JIM: "I can see this is important to get out as quickly as possible, but it's impossible to do it by Friday. I'd like to do it for you, but Wednesday is the earliest time I can get it out, and only by putting two extra people on it."

KENT: "What if I OKed four extra people from Tim's group to work on it? Could it be done by Friday?"

JIM: "We might be able to do it with four extra people plus your OK of overtime if we need it."

KENT: "You got it!"

JIM: "I'll get the people on it right now."

The persistent response may be used appropriately to deal with people who ask you for information you're not able to give them, things you don't have the authority to give, or favors that regulations forbid. It can also be used in your personal life to handle door-to-door and telephone salespeople or in any other situation in which you feel someone is trying to manipulate you.

SUMMARY

This chapter focused on the need to be able to say no in order to be in charge of your work force. You completed an assessment that assisted you in identifying your problem area. The say-no techniques of the assertive, passive, and aggressive supervisory styles were examined.

Guidelines were provided to assist you in saying no assertively. You learned eight ways to say no. The persistent response was explained as a technique for handling manipulation, unreasonable requests, and extremely aggressive people.

9 Handling Criticism

It's so easy to see both sides of an issue when we are not particularly concerned about it.

Unknown

It's discouraging to make a mistake, but it's downright humiliating to find out you're so unimportant nobody even noticed it.

Unknown

Being able to handle criticism is a definite step toward being fully in charge of yourself. Because criticism often includes blame and judgment, it may lead to feeling victimized and defensive. The problem with defensive behavior is that it cuts the other person off, which usually intensifies the situation. The purpose of this chapter is to expand your understanding of criticism and to give you a variety of responses to assist you in coping with criticism directed at you.

REASONS CRITICISM IS HARD TO HANDLE

The Conditioning Process

Probably the most significant reason people are oversensitive to criticism is the impact of their past conditioning. How you were criticized as a child influences how you handle criticism today.

Many parents seem to be caught up in "parenting by exceptions"— what goes wrong is what they pay attention to. As a result, mistakes are pointed out far more often than positive behaviors are responded to. To add to the problem, the criticism is usually stated with the you-blaming approach and the attitude that if someone makes a mistake, there is something wrong with that person. Thus, the behavior is not separated from the person. The natural tendency of children, then, is to identify with the judgmental label *bad, wrong,* and *dumb.* This identification is carried into adult life, which leaves people fearing rejection while finding it difficult to separate their mistakes from themselves.

EXERCISE 9.1

Self-Awareness Exercise: Handling Criticism

To learn how your past has influenced your ability to handle criticism, complete the following exercise.

Past Experiences

1. When you did something your parents thought was bad or wrong, what did they do?

2. How did they tell you about it?

3. What did you do in response to what they said or did?

4. How did you feel?

Accepting Criticism

1. When you do something your boss thinks is bad or wrong, what does he or she do?

2. How does he or she tell you about it?

3. What do you do in response to what he or she says or does?

4. How do you feel?

Offering Criticism

1. When one of your employees does something you judge as bad or wrong, what do you so and say?

2. Do you express your criticism with the you-blaming approach or with the I-rational approach?

3. If you use the you-blaming approach, how can you modify your critical statements into I-rational terms?

4. What else might you do to modify your attitude so that you can handle the problem in the assertive style?

Discussion of Exercise 9.1

As you completed this exercise, you probably discovered that your childhood conditioning has affected both how you handle criticism and how you offer it. Remember that most people have had little or no training in how to respond to mistakes with the I-rational approach. The assertive supervision attitude toward mistakes is that "my mistakes are to be corrected and learned from" and "one of the quickest ways to lose my self-confidence is to let others be my judge."

HANDLING CRITICISM AND THE THREE SUPERVISORY STYLES

The Passive Supervisor

Passive supervisors usually fear rejection, which leads to feelings of anxiety and low self-esteem. They often judge what people say in terms of their own feelings of worthlessness. They are unconsciously driven by the need to please others at their own expense.

Passive supervisors often deny their errors through defensiveness or apologetically seek forgiveness, or they try somehow to make up for the mistake. They "yes people to death" when they are criticized but fail to formulate any plan of action to deal with the problem. In the end, it is difficult for others to depend on them because no one knows if they will carry out their yesses.

Passive supervisors assume others know best and elevate others to positions of authority. These supervisors automatically become guilty when they make mistakes, which leads to their being vulnerable to periods of resentment and depression. Often people decide not to approach them in order to avoid feeling responsible for lowering the supervisor's self-esteem—even though they aren't truly responsible for the supervisor's feelings. The sad outcome is that because these supervisors won't take criticism in its proper perspective, they lose the valuable insights it may provide.

The Aggressive Supervisor

People often bounce from the passive to the aggressive mode when reacting to criticism. When supervisors don't have the skills to handle criticism effectively, they may respond defensively or counterattack, as if to say, "I'm not OK–you're not OK either . . . so there!" Needless to say, this reaction creates ill will, endangers further cooperation, and often causes a big argument.

Aggressive supervisors react quickly to criticism, without evaluating the criticism to find out if it's true or not. Like passive supervisors, aggressive supervisors are often seen as unapproachable. Often, others will not criticize them openly because of their emotional, critical reactions. They scare people off by their angry judgmental reactions.

This results in their losing out on honest feedback and constructive suggestions from those with whom they work. Even though they do *not* react aggressively *every* time, most people assume they will. The sad outcome is that they will lose out on valuable information about themselves that could lead to professional growth.

The Assertive Supervisor

Assertive supervisors have the confidence to deal with criticism effectively. They can discriminate between unjust and just criticism. They are aware of situations in which they react poorly to criticism and have a plan of action to help them respond more effectively the next time around. They have learned to desensitize themselves to critical remarks. As a result, their ability to handle criticism improves along with their sense of dignity and self-respect.

They believe that human beings make mistakes and that they have a right to make mistakes and learn from them. They are aware that it is natural and unavoidable to experience occasional rejection. Having the belief that they are not responsible for the way others react and feel helps them deal with criticisms objectively and calmly. They often meet the critic halfway by asking themselves pertinent questions, such as:

Why is this person making this criticism?

What is he or she attempting to say?

What would be the best way to solve the problem?

Assertive supervisors value those who bring mistakes and oversights to their attention. In their work groups, everyone has the right to approach the supervisor about an error or to provide critical suggestions.

CASE *Bob, a supervisor for a large manufacturing company, illustrates the importance of being open to critical feedback:

"I was once saved from what could have been a very embarrassing situation by a newly hired assistant. Several senior members of my staff had prepared a special report for my presentation at a high-level departmental meeting. I thought

---

*Adapted from *How to Ask for a Raise Without Getting Fired*, by Larry Schwimmer (New York: Harper and Row, 1981).

the report was well-organized and competently done. I had told everyone in my department I was looking forward to presenting the results of the report at the meeting later that day.

"Later on, this newly hired assistant asked to speak to me in my office: 'Bob, it's about that report. I know you think it is done well. And I know I am new around here. So I feel a little hesitant and uncomfortable being critical about it. But I want to say that, after reviewing it, I feel that it has a couple of sales statistics that appear to be incorrect, resulting in some erroneous conclusions. I've brought the quarterly report with me and would like to go over it with you to show you where I think there has been a mistake.'

"Well, sure enough, when we went through the numbers, there were two glaring mistakes that probably had been made when the report was originally tabulated. These errors in turn resulted in the wrong conclusions. I couldn't help thinking what a fool I would have looked like in front of the other department heads, since the error would have been quickly noticed on close scrutiny.

"I owe that assistant a real debt of gratitude for having the courage to speak up. As a new addition to the department, it would have been easy for her to stay silent. She could have thought, 'After all, I'm new here, I'd better keep my mouth shut.' When I approached her to thank her personally, she said that, while it had been difficult to bring the matter to my attention, she felt that she could approach me—so she did."

As an assertive supervisor, Bob was approachable, a quality that paid real dividends in that incident.

EXERCISE 9.2   ## Self-Assessment: How Do I Handle Criticism?

The following behavioral statements regarding dealing with criticism will assist you in determining how sensitive you are to different types of criticism. Be as honest in your assessment of yourself as you would be about your best friend. Assess the statements as follows: Put a plus (+) by those you feel you handle assertively. Put a zero (0) by those you avoid handling. Put an X by those you face but handle poorly.

Assessment   *Behavior Statement*

_____ 1. Your boss criticizes you about a fault that you do have—one you deny.

_____ 2. You express an honest criticism to an employee about his performance.

_____ 3. A peer criticizes you for something you know is untrue.

_____ 4. An employee has put you down in an indirect way. There may be a little truth to the putdown; however, it's more untrue than true.

_____ 5. A peer criticizes you about a fault that you do have—one that you can't deny.

_____ 6. Things have not been going your way lately, and you are feeling a lack of self-confidence. Your manager criticizes you for "being down."

_____ 7. Your boss criticizes you for something you know is untrue.

_____ 8. Another supervisor has critically pointed out a mistake you made. You agree with her judgment.

_____ 9. A peer has just told you that your point of view is just plain stupid.

Discussion of Exercise 9.2

In the space given, note the situations that you handled poorly or avoided handling. These are situations that you want to handle more effectively:

The nine situations in Exercise 9.2 are the result of the author's informal survey of about 200 people. The survey question was "What kind of situations that happen on the job do you have the most difficulty handling?" These nine situations were mentioned most often. The remainder of this chapter contains various responses you can use to handle these problems.

TECHNIQUES FOR HANDLING CRITICISM EFFECTIVELY

Be Your Own Best Critic

Knowing the areas of yourself on which you can improve will go a long way in helping you deal with those criticisms that are true or partially true. Criticisms strike at your ego and self-esteem. One of the best ways to handle the criticisms is to be fully aware of the components of yourself that result in self-defeating behavior. If you are aware that awareness will diminish the possibility of shock, hurt, or defensiveness.

Jim, a supervisor at a bank, is an example of a person aware of his shortcomings. The following is a dialogue between Jim and his manager, Jennifer.

JENNIFER: "Jim, the weekly statistical reports you have been turning in have mathematical errors in them consistently."

JIM: (He knows that the criticism is valid, yet he feels embarrassed at having made such mistakes. He feels angry at himself that his reaction is to get defensive and upset. By arguing with Jennifer or coming up with a list of *excuses,* all Jim will accomplish is to escalate the issue. However, as a professional, he will focus on being objective about his self-defeating behavior and get to work on a solution so that the problem will not continue—nor the criticism.) "Jennifer, you're right about the errors. So from now on, in order to make sure that the reports will be fully accurate, I will have one of my co-workers read the numbers as a final check."

Guidelines for Accepting Criticism

Separate yourself from the criticism. You are not your mistakes.

It's OK to dislike your behavior and still like yourself.

Think about modifying and improving your behavior, not labeling or judging yourself.

Deal with the issue, not your personality or irrelevant personal matters.

Hold the belief that *you,* not others, are responsible for your behavior and feelings.

Applying these guidelines the next time you are criticized will help you accept the criticism more effectively.

Requesting Negative Feedback

Another approach in handling criticism is to *request* negative feedback. Solicit criticism in order to improve and perfect your performance. When you do, listen to the criticism from the other person's point of view. Ask clarifying questions related to the data on which the criticism is based, such as:

"I don't understand. What is it about . . . that could be improved?"

"What did I do that . . . ?"

"What is it about what I'm doing that . . . ?

"What am I doing specifically that . . . ?"

"How did I do . . . that was incorrect?"

"Is this all you can think of now that I could do to improve my performance?"

These questions will assist you in staying focused on the issue and the data on which the criticism is based. Unless you understand the data, it is difficult to determine whether the criticism is just or unjust. Remember to stay in the I'm OK–You're OK position, which helps you be non-judgmental. When you do this, you empower yourself. There is a lot of satisfaction in not letting the other person "hook you."

Identifying the Types of Criticism

Recognizing the kind of criticism that is being directed at you will help you decide on the most appropriate response. Criticisms usually fall into one of three categories:

1. Unjustified criticisms expressed in broad and general terms, unrealistic and opposed to the truth. For example:

   "You're *always* late (when you've been late three times in two years).

   "You *never* prepare your reports properly" (when you did one report incorrectly).

   "*Every* time you are told about an error, you get defensive" (when you were defensive twice in the last six months).

   "You *never* tell me you appreciate my work" (when you expressed your appreciation to this employee three times during the week).

   Keep in mind you don't behave one way *every single time*. Watch out for words like *always, never, all the time,* or *every time* because they state your behavior in absolute terms. Avoid accepting such criticism at face value.

   The following responses could be used to deal with this type of criticism:

   "I understand how you might perceive me that way. My perception is . . . (then state what your perception is).

   "That may be true. I don't see myself that way."

   You can also respond with an empathetic listening statement; for example, in response to "You never tell me you appreciate my work," you could reply: "It sounds like you feel I'm not giving you the appreciation you expect. Could you give me an example of how this happens?" In response to "You never prepare your reports properly," you could say: "It seems you are displeased with the way I completed the last report. What specifically did I do that you found incorrect?"

2. A criticism that has an element of truth in it but is stated aggressively. A possible response to this type of criticism is the *turnaround:*

"You could be right about that."

"You might be right about . . ."

"You're probably right about . . ."

"What you say makes sense."

The object of these responses is not to deny, not to get defensive, not to counterattack with your own criticism, but to turn the critical remark around so you are in charge. By using this type of response, you offer no resistance so that the other person no longer has something to push against. This allows you to move into focusing on the issue and solving the difficulty. By using these responses, you acknowledge the criticism as partly valid. You may add a statement about how you are working on doing something to change your behavior.

These kinds of responses actually reduce the frequency of criticisms. They prompt the critic to be assertive, which is what you want. This approach desensitizes you to criticism. By not reacting defensively to the criticism, you are able to handle it calmly and effectively.

The following dialogue is an example of a supervisor seeking a raise and prompting criticism of her work using turnarounds, clarifying, and empathetic listening responses.

SUSAN: "HARRY, what is your reason for not recommending me for a merit raise?"

HARRY: "It's simple—you don't deserve it."

SUSAN: "I don't understand, Harry. What did I do that was unmeritorious?"

HARRY: "Well, for one thing, you're new on the job. Less than six months, right?"

SUSAN: "Right."

HARRY: "You haven't had the time to learn all the ropes yet. You're not doing bad. You're just average."

SUSAN: "What am I doing that makes me just average?"

HARRY: "You're making all the typical mistakes that a new supervisor makes."

SUSAN: "What am I doing specifically that are typical mistakes?"

HARRY: "A couple of things. Like, for instance, the sales-forecasting project for the Jenson account."

SUSAN: "OK. How did I go wrong on that one?"

HARRY: "You underestimated sales by $3,000. We lost the account because of your errors."

SUSAN: "You're right. I didn't check my figures out with one of the more experienced supervisors or maybe even you."

HARRY: "Don't worry about it. We all make mistakes, and you are going to have your share of them."

SUSAN: "Anything else I'm doing that's just average and I could improve?"

HARRY: "A couple of other things."

SUSAN: "Let's hear them."

HARRY: "You're still a bit slow in getting the work in."

SUSAN: "I'm taking too much time?"

HARRY: "No, not too much time. Just average for your experience."

SUSAN: "Anything else?"

HARRY: "One more thing that I can think of—when you turn in your statistics, make sure you put them in the order I suggested yesterday because it's easier to read."

SUSAN: "Is that all you can think of now that makes me just average?"

HARRY: "Yeah, that sounds like it."

SUSAN: "And I could speed things up without making more mistakes that cost money?"

HARRY: "Yup."

SUSAN: "And I could be more careful of the neatness of the work I turn in?"

HARRY: "That sounds about right."

SUSAN: "Well, I want a crack at the merit list next time. I'd like to go over some of the things I may have doubts about with you. Since I have to improve, I want to do it as fast as possible."

HARRY: "Sure."

3. A criticism that is valid and stated in a straightforward manner in an attempt to improve your behavior.

The best possible response to these criticisms is admitting your mistakes or shortcomings, like this:

"You're right. I did do that incorrectly. Now that I know the correct way to do it, I will complete it correctly."

"You're right. I probably didn't think that through carefully. Do you have a suggestion as to how I could improve?"

"I've noticed that myself. My plan is to improve in that area. I could use any ideas that you might have."

"You're right. I didn't like the way I did that either."

One final comment: It is important to consider the mood of the person who is criticizing you. It may be that he or she is under the gun from those above, or has had a pet project turned down, or has been given a tough new directive by the boss. Consider the critic's frame of mind as well as the nature of the behavior.

Assertive Statements for Use in Handling Criticism

The following are additional responses to be used in various situations at your discretion.

1. To help keep your cool, ask the other person to restate what he or she said or ask a question: "What is it about the way I did the assignment that you don't like?"

2. In response to, "Yes, but it's . . .": "What I hear you saying is all the reasons why it won't work. I'd like us both to operate with open minds. Let's look at how to implement this and the ways it could be effectively completed."

3. "I want to work this out with you."

4. When someone says something with which you don't agree: "Fine, we have a different perspective."

5. When "yessing" is being done out of hostility: "I get the sense that you are saying yes out of anger and you don't agree with me."

6. "I'm not comfortable with or willing to listen to evasiveness."

7. "I want to make sure I understand what you are saying."

8. "How would you solve or take care of this situation?"

9. "Are you interested in working this out with me?"

10. "It seems that I'm not completely aware of what is happening."

11. "If you are not willing to work out this agreement with me, what is your suggestion as to how we could solve this problem?"

12. Summarize what has been said, state the objective, and set a time limit.

13. "I think you have a right to your doubts."

14. "I want to explain my reasons for . . ."

15. "I want to create an environment between us where we can talk about what is going on."

16. "I understand your feelings. What I am interested in is discussing with you what I am unhappy about and the results I expect."

17. "I feel frustrated that we're not able to work this out or discuss it."

18. "I think you have a right to view my behavior from your perspective. However, I don't share your perspective. I will be willing to listen to specific examples."

Many people find that combining responses works well. Review the 18 responses and put a check by those you feel would work best with the difficult people with whom you interact. To help you respond to these people and incorporate these responses, write a script. Include in the script what they say, what response to use, what they might say to your response, and, finally, how you would respond. Visualize the interaction the way you have written it. Stand in front of a mirror and say your response so you can see and hear how you come across. To help you even more, practice the script with a friend. The best way to incorporate a new behavior is to visualize it or do it. Have fun with this. You'll be surprised at the positive results.

EXERCISE 9.3   **Practice in Handling Criticism**

This exercise will give you an opportunity to practice using the responses suggested in this chapter. Examine the critical remarks given and develop an appropriate response. Then compare your answers to those at the end of the exercise.

1. Your boss says: "Look at all these mistakes. I can't believe you did this! I guess I gave you too much credit. You really let me down."

   Response:

2. You do an excellent job overall but are periodically careless, making some obvious mistakes. You are criticized by your manager: "Sandy, you constantly make such dumb mistakes on these reports. You know how much I count on you. Why can't you be more careful?"
   Response:

3. You are at an important staff meeting. Without turning off the members of the group who have stated strong opinions, you want to get the group to adopt your sales ideas. Terry thinks your ideas are ridiculous. He says, "Billie, you can't be serious about that proposal. That's totally absurd! You know that it will fail. Just listen to my idea."
Response:

4. Your boss criticizes you for something you know without a doubt you didn't do.
Response:

Possible Responses:

1. "It appears I've made an error that really upsets you. What specifically have I done that you feel let down about?"

2. "I understand your feelings. It sounds like you feel I've let you down, even though you count on me not to make careless mistakes. I've decided to have one of my staff go over future reports with me so this kind of thing doesn't continue."

3. "Terry, it's apparent that you and I have different points of view on the best way to handle this situation. I'll listen to yours, and perhaps we can explore how our ideas can be combined to best advantage."

4. "I'm puzzled by your critical comment. I don't perceive myself doing this. Would you give me an example of how I do this?"

As you did this practice exercise, you probably became aware of the importance of stating these responses in an assertive style and the OK-OK attitude. Your voice tone, inflection, facial expression, and body posture will also help determine how these responses are perceived by the other person.

SUMMARY

In this chapter, you saw how your childhood conditioning influences your ability to handle criticism. Because people identify themselves with the criticisms, they find it difficult to separate their behavior from themselves. You completed a self-awareness exercise to help you become aware of how your past influences your present ability to handle criticism.

You learned how the must-be directives (please others, be perfect, be strong, try hard, hurry up) make it hard to handle criticisms assertively. Must-be directives often lead to the passive and aggressive styles and the not-OK attitudes. This behavior causes ill feelings and arguments and leaves issues unresolved. You developed a plan of action to modify non-productive behavior using the A→B→C→D belief model and the visualization process.

The passive, aggressive, and assertive approaches to handling criticisms were examined and contrasted. The assertive approach leads to effective handling of criticisms, while the passive and aggressive approaches do not.

The completion of the self-assessment on how you handle criticism helped you identify specifically the areas you handle assertively and those you react to aggressively and passively.

Techniques and approaches for handling criticism effectively were covered. You learned that self-knowledge can assist you in defusing your emotional responses. By being your own best critic, following the guidelines for handling criticism, requesting negative feedback, using clarifying questions, identifying the types of criticisms with which you are dealing, responding with turnarounds, and admitting your mistakes and shortcomings, you can handle criticism objectively, calmly, and effectively. You were given additional assertive statements and nondirective statements to add to your repertoire of responses, which will allow you to be more flexible and versatile in dealing with criticism.

10 Giving and Receiving Positive Feedback

General Eisenhower used to demonstrate the art of leadership with a simple piece of string. He'd put it on a table and say: "Pull it and it'll follow wherever you wish. Push it and it will go nowhere at all. It's that way when it comes to leading people."

Unknown

There is no such thing as an unmotivated person.

Charles A. Coonradt, "The Game of War"

People have a way of becoming what you encourage them to be, not what you nag them to be.

Unknown

A research organization polled 500 executives, asking them what traits they thought were most important in dealing with others. From the information received, five basic "rules" were formulated. They are:

1. Give your people the credit that is rightfully theirs. To do otherwise is both morally and ethically dishonest.

2. Be courteous. Have genuine consideration for other people's feelings, wishes, and problems.

3. Don't tamper with the truth. Don't rationalize. What you might *like* to believe is not necessarily the truth.

4. Be concise in your writing and talking, especially when giving instructions to others.

5. Be generous. Remember that it is the productivity of others that makes possible your executive position.

The above five rules are excellent tips to aid you in being a more effective leader. As you can see, these executives placed a high value on positive feedback and how it is given. The "how" is the crucial ingredient. More than likely you have discovered this for yourself. The question often is, "How do I do it better?" or "What is the correct and/or best way?" You'll notice that the quotation from General Eisenhower strongly indicates his belief in regard to this issue—pushing people, "the how," is not motivating them to initiate action on their own accord.

A major part of your job as a supervisor is human relations. Human relations is not just good "horse sense"; it involves more than responding to people instinctively. Everyday activities are full of paradoxes and inconsistencies, so that good intentions and straight-line reasoning are often not enough. Each person you supervise handles situations differently and is motivated differently. So to effectively handle this human relations aspect of your job, it's important to realize that knowing *why* people do things before you can predict *what* they will do will help you be more effective. Motives and needs are the underlying factors in why people behave the way they do. Knowing what a person's needs are will assist you in motivating that person.

EXERCISE 10.1   ## Case Study in Motivation

To begin being more aware of the phenomenon of people being motivated differently, take a moment to examine the following on-the-job situation and answer the questions that follow.

Dean Anderson supervises Jim and Bob, who work side by side on an assembly line in an auto plant. Their job is to attach the garnish (or trim) to the painted body. For some time, Jim and Bob have been complaining of nicks and cuts received from handling the sharp pieces of metal. Finally, Dean decides that the best way to cure the problem is to insist that both men wear gloves on the job.

On Monday, Dean approaches Jim and Bob together. "Guys," says Dean, "the safety department has approved the issuance of work gloves for this job. This should prevent the rash of cuts you've been getting. Here's a pair of gloves for each of you. From now on, I'll expect to see you wearing them all the time."

Next day, Dean has to ask Jim to put his gloves on three separate times. Bob wears his all the time. At week's end, Bob is sold on the value of gloves. But Jim just sticks his in his pants pocket. "They slow me down, so I can't keep up with the line," he tells Dean. But to Bob he says, "This work glove idea is just an excuse to justify speeding up the line. If you give in on this issue, they'll put the boots to you on the next."

1. What do you think is going on that these two men handled the same situation in such different ways?

2. What supervisory style do you see Dean following?

   Assertive _____ Passive _____ Aggressive _____

   Why?

3. Based on the information in this book, how would a supervisor deal with this situation using the assertive supervisory approach?

Discussion of Exercise 10.1

Supervisors behaving assertively would have included the two men in coming up with a solution. They would have operated from the choice principle. When people are part of the process to make decisions and come up with solutions, they have more vested interest in making the solution work. This is part of the principle of choice: When people have choices about what they do, they are more motivated. By asking Jim and Bob for their ideas and feelings and getting them involved in the problem-solving process, Dean would have increased the possibilities that Jim would be wearing gloves.

The above case study also illustrates the importance of understanding the "whys" and "whats" of those you supervise. If you know that Martinson dislikes his job because it requires concentration, you can make a good guess that Martinson will make it hard for you to change the job by increasing its complexity. If Susan works in your unit because of the conversations she has with her co-workers, you can predict that Susan will be unhappy if she's assigned to an isolated spot.

The goal of this chapter is to provide you with a better understanding of why people have difficulty receiving and giving feedback and ways to receive and give positive feedback.

RECEIVING POSITIVE FEEDBACK

How the Conditioning Process Inhibits Receiving Positive Feedback

Being uncomfortable receiving compliments is directly related to the kinds of messages people received as children. Often these messages leave no doubt in children's minds that they must be "modest" and that it is "wrong" to say nice things about themselves.

The result is that these messages can harm people's self-esteem and self-worth and make it not-OK to accept positive feedback graciously. People often believe that it is immodest to acknowledge a compliment. Children are often directed, when complimented, to respond by putting the compliment down, protesting, or showing embarrassment. The adverse consequence is that the one giving the compliment feels put down or uneasy for having "said the wrong thing." A natural tendency is to avoid giving compliments to that person in the future. Even though the person wanted the compliment, the negative response influences others to stop giving compliments.

If you have difficulty accepting positive feedback, examine your behavior using the A→B→C→D belief model; then change your self-defeating belief to a more positive one.

Responses to Compliments: The following statements, to be used in response to compliments, can assist you in this area. The main point is to get a "thank you" out, or at least a smile or nod of acknowledgment, no matter what. If need be, use the visualization technique described in previous chapters, or practice with a friend or peer so that you can feel comfortable using these responses at the time you receive a compliment.

"Thank you."

"Thank you! I appreciate your comment."

"Thank you! I like hearing that."

"Thank you! I like it that you noticed."

"Thank you! I think so too (or *I like it too*)."

Smile or nod in acknowledgment.

"Thank you!" then make a statement expanding on what the other said.

The following dialogue shows that Lorraine knows how to receive a compliment.

TORRANCE (Manager): "Lorraine, I liked the way you said no to that salesperson. You didn't beat around the bush or let him talk you into buying supplies you don't need."

LORRAINE (Supervisor): "Thanks, Torrance, it has taken me a while to learn how to say no assertively. I'm beginning to have confidence in that area. I appreciate your noticing."

Responding graciously to positive feedback has certain advantages for you:

You will have increased self-esteem.

You will have improved self-image.

Other people will feel good complimenting you.

You will get more compliments because you handle them well.

You will feel empowered.

You will project yourself as a professional.

You will find it easier to compliment others.

You will experience less stress and tension.

You will have more energy.

You will experience positive feelings more often.

You probably can think of other advantages. If so, take some time to note them here.

The One-Up/One-Down Relationship

Supervisors often say, "Why does my manager give positive feedback so rarely?" The main reason is that your manager gets caught up in paying attention to what goes wrong. Like you, managers are expected to keep their eyes out for errors, then to correct them. Thus the natural tendency is to be critical—to crack down on you for things that go wrong.

Many managers don't realize or forget that criticism doesn't motivate you as well as positive feedback. With criticism, if you work harder, it's because you "have to." However, with positive feedback, you work harder because you "want to," and most often you will do much more.

If you are not getting the feedback you want, it is important that you take the initiative and set up a meeting to assert your wants. The following are a few statements you could use to initiate this meeting:

> "Jim, I've noticed that you and I haven't discussed your evaluation of me in some time. When do you have time for this?"

> "Carol, I'm experiencing a lack of feedback from you about my performance. I want to meet with you to discuss this."

> "Darrell, getting feedback from you about how I'm doing is important to me. I haven't gotten it for some time. I'd like us to plan a time when we can talk about how you perceive my performance."

An important dimension of your relationship with your boss is its one-up/one-down aspect. This relationship is pictured in Figure 10.1.

Interplay of the One-Up/One-Down Relationship

The behavioral style—assertive, passive, aggressive—in which you spend most of your time while interacting with your boss will influence how effective or ineffective the association is. Supervisors who are in the passive mode seem to have the most difficulty because they are caught up in pleasing others. They spend a lot of their time "trying" to behave in a manner that is pleasing to their boss. Often they feel anxious about behaving "right" according to their manager's criteria. They are so busy taking care of the boss's needs that they lose track of their own. When they do become aware that their own needs aren't being met, they become depressed, resentful, frustrated, and angry and blame the boss for these feelings and for the position in which they put themselves by *not* asserting themselves. Because they have low self-esteem and a self-concept that doesn't include behaving assertively, they withhold their feelings and ideas. They perceive being assertive as high-risk behavior and will even catastrophize that if they did speak up, they'd be fired. Thus, they deprive their boss of needed information that could be helpful in getting the job done more efficiently.

Assertive supervisors know the value of expressing their ideas and feelings in order to keep communication open between themselves and their bosses. Because they have high self-esteem, they behave naturally and appropriately for the situation.

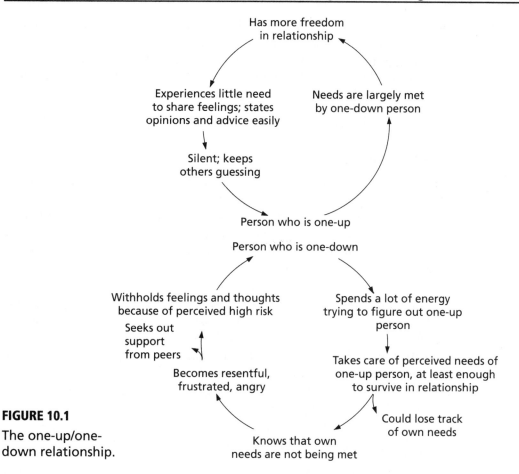

FIGURE 10.1

The one-up/one-down relationship.

How Supervisors from the Assertive-Passive-Aggressive Styles Receive Positive Feedback

The following illustrations will provide you with a clearer understanding of how supervisors from each of the supervisory styles deal with receiving positive feedback.

Passive Style

Stephen is a supervisor for a small manufacturing plant in the Midwest. Instead of taking care of his own needs, Stephen compulsively takes care of others and makes them feel good at his own expense. He uses compliments to cheer his employees up rather than taking the risk that they may express negative feelings that he would have difficulty handling. As a consequence, negative feelings are kept under cover, leading to tension and unresolved problems. When he does receive a compliment,

Stephen feels obliged to return it. He is uncomfortable receiving compliments because he doesn't think he's *that* good. You would hear him say in response to compliments such things as: "It wasn't much, really," "It was mainly luck," or "I could have done a lot better." Although Stephen gets along well enough with others, he feels out of control much of the time.

Aggressive Style

Anne, on the other hand, makes sure that she is in control at all times. Anne has a high opinion of herself; thus she expects to receive positive feedback. When it doesn't come, she makes others not-OK for not telling her how good she is. Since she isn't concerned about people, she uses praise to manipulate others to get what she wants. She's able to turn off sincerity like water from a faucet—on when she want something, off when she gets what she wants.

The outcome is that her employees are suspicious when she goes out of her way to "be nice to them" because they assume she's after something. She will use praise as a gimmick to try to get employees to change their behavior. This effort to control them in this way results in feelings of resentment, frustration, and anger. Over the short haul, Anne gets results; but over a long period of time, the negative feelings result in low morale, alienation, and high turnover.

Assertive Style

Sharon, on the other hand, regards compliments as a sincere, specific expression of appreciation. She will acknowledge what the other person has said verbally or nonverbally with a nod or smile of acceptance. And, if it is appropriate, she offers free feedback regarding how she feels about what was said. Sharon expresses appreciation freely and constructively in a truthful and straightforward manner, in much the same way she provides constructive criticism. Since she has the interests of others at heart, she builds a reservoir of goodwill. She doesn't have to advertise the fact that she is sincere—it's visible in the things she does and how she does them.

It is clear from these three examples that each supervisory style has distinct ways to handle compliments. It is evident that supervisors' beliefs about themselves strongly influence how they behave in the area of handling compliments.

GIVING POSITIVE FEEDBACK

CASE   A certain chief executive, who has done an amazing job of transforming a run-down company into an outstanding success, instructs each supervisor to submit every Monday morning a report of all the *good* things that have happened in his or her work group during the preceding week.

You depend heavily on the effectiveness of your employees, and the manner in which your unit works together effectively is largely due to how you apply positive feedback. One way to increase your effectiveness is to understand how vital positive feedback is to your employees.

Strokes

The first aspect of human behavior that you will examine is the influence of the conditioning process on people's needs for attention and recognition. Dr. Eric Berne, the creator of Transaction Analysis, describes attention and recognition as "strokes."* Strokes can be negative or positive; they can be given physically, nonverbally, and verbally. If a stroke is given because of what a person does, it is considered a conditional stroke: It is earned, and there are strings attached. For example, if Irene, an employee, gets her work done on time, her supervisor could give her a positive, verbal conditional stroke. On the other hand, if Irene comes to work late, the supervisor could give her a negative, verbal conditional stroke.

Another kind of stroke is an unconditional stroke. Unconditional strokes are strokes for "being." No strings are attached, and they aren't earned. When you approach an employee for no particular reason and say that you like having him or her as an employee, you have given a positive, verbal unconditional stroke.

Everyone needs to be recognized and to have attention paid to them. It is extremely important for you as a supervisor to respond to this need. How you stroke those you supervise will strongly influence how effectively your group will work together. Two mottos to keep in mind are:

"What you stroke is what you get." This means that if you stroke negative behavior, you are, in fact, rewarding it. The negative behavior to which you are paying attention will more than likely continue.

***Games People Play*, by Eric Berne, Ph.D. (Ballantine, 1978).

"Negative strokes are better than none." If you don't stroke employees in a positive manner to a degree that fits their needs, you'll probably perpetuate negative behavior. Since humans need attention, if they aren't getting it through the positive things they do, they will do something negative to get attention.

These two mottos have strong implications in terms of motivation and productivity for yourself and those you supervise.

There are four major categories of consequences of behavior to keep in mind.

1. An individual receives something pleasant—a positive stroke such as a raise, recognition, a smile, or encouragement.

2. An individual has something unpleasant taken away—a positive stroke such as a distasteful task or a repetitious task.

3. An individual receives something unpleasant—a negative stroke such as a cut in pay, a putdown, demerits, or criticism.

4. An individual has something pleasant taken away—a negative stroke such as a fun assignment, working with something enjoyable, or a cheerful greeting.

When you are having difficulty understanding why an employee is doing something unpleasant, ask yourself, "What is that individual accomplishing by that activity?" "What is he or she getting out of it?" More than likely, you will find out that what he or she is getting out of it is attention—negative attention, perhaps, but don't forget: Negative strokes are better than none.

A wide variety of positive and negative strokes can be given on the job. There can be positive strokes that acknowledge employees and lead to motivation and improved self-esteem, or negative strokes that can demotivate and lower self-esteem. The tables on the following pages show positive and negative strokes broken down into three categories: physical, verbal, and nonverbal.

Positive

How might people respond to being stroked positively? They might:

- Increase their productivity

- Feel secure, satisfied, appreciated, contented, happy, accepted

Physical	Verbal	Nonverbal
Touch on the arm or shoulder	Statement of appreciation	Effective listening
Pat on the back	Thank you	Concern
Handshake	First-name recognition	Positive facial expression
Statement of appreciation	Encouragement	Smile
	Recognition of achievement	Warmth
	Solicit, hear opinion	Attentiveness
	Request for input regarding a suggestion	Written compliment
	Compliment	Award
		Gift
		Relaxed, open posture
		Eye contact
		Belonging to a group
		Being given a choice
		Being part of solving a problem

- Think positively about themselves and others

- Continue to perform well and improve

- Feel empowered

- Have a feeling of belonging and being needed and important

- Have improved self-esteem

- Find it easier to behave assertively and in the OK-OK mode

- Be more motivated and responsive

- Take more interest in the work

- Feel increased enthusiasm, higher morale

- Feel enhanced mutual respect and cooperation

- Tend to want to stroke others positively

- Feel more confident and, therefore, perform better

- Work better as a team

- Exhibit less turnover, absenteeism, illness

Negative

How might people respond to being stroked in this manner? They might:

Physical	Verbal	Nonverbal
Shove	Judgmental criticism	Ignoring suggestions
Punch, hit, slap	Negative labels	Critical facial expression: frown, rolling eyes
	Ridicule	
	Belittling remarks, put-downs	Pointed finger
	Unjust condemnation	Not listening
	Dictating orders	Indifference, unconcerned attitude
	Name calling	
	Yelling	Tapping foot, pencil, finger
	Abusive language	Not responding, looking away
	Using accusing phrases	
	Reprimands	Closed, rigid posture
		Very little lattitude, work within constrictions

- Feel indifferent

- Have a careless attitude, lack effort

- Feel insecure, discouraged, inadequate

- Be nonmotivated, decrease production

- Exhibit low morale, absenteeism, high turnover, more illness

- Have an attitude of "I don't give a damn!"

- Have a feeling of not belonging

- Have lowered self-esteem

- Feel hostility, anger, depression, rebellion, resentment

- Exhibit decreased initiative, trust, pride in work

- Show discontent, disinterest, apathy

- Say "Who cares?" "Why try!" "They don't like me," "They're picking on me," "I'll get even," "They think I'm dumb."

- Have low self-esteem, feel inferior

Napoleon once observed, "An army's effectiveness depends on its size, training, experience, and morale . . . and morale is worth more than all the other factors combined." The same is true in every organization. No matter how capable a person is, when morale sags, so does performance.

It's not hard to spot low morale: The zest goes out of a person's work, the loss of interest and enthusiasm is apparent, and it shows in decreased effort and poor results.

People can become disenchanted with their jobs for any number of reasons. Figuring out why takes a willingness to talk and listen to your work group, to observe what bothers them, to read between the lines, and to check out your conclusions with them.

Good pay is important to morale, but it's just a part of the story. The most vital thing is the knowledge that one's boss cares about him or her as a person, not just as a means of turning out work. When people know that their boss is genuinely interested in them, their feelings, their problems, and their ambitions, positive attitudes usually follow.

You aren't in a position to give your work group everything they want all the time. However, you can be aware of what people want, show them that you know how they feel, and satisfy their wants whenever you can. Doing this consistently and sincerely will make for high morale in your unit.

| **EXERCISE 10.2** | **Stroking** |

Now that you have had some practice in identifying the various kinds of positive and negative strokes, complete this exercise.

1. Pick a person on the job with whom you are having some problems. It could be someone you supervise, your boss, a peer, or a person from another department. Write the name of the person you choose:

2. What does this person do to get your attention—to get stroked by you, either positively or negatively? List what he or she does (behavior, action, characteristics):

3. For each behavior or characteristic listed, note how you respond and which kind of stroke—positive or negative—you give.

4. From which behavior do you respond to the person: aggressive, passive, or assertive?

What behavior is the person in most often?

5. What positive action could you take to change the interactive pattern between the two of you to a more positive one?

6. What would an assertive supervisor do?

7. What are you willing to do to resolve the problem and find a solution?

Discussion of Exercise 10.2

Changing or modifying a negative relationship between yourself and another person can take time and energy. It is important to understand that if you are having a problem with another, you are part of the problem. If you weren't, there wouldn't be a problem. One of the most significant ideas you can learn is this: There aren't any problems, only people that make them. Think about it the next time you're having a problem. You'll be amazed to realize that if you had a different belief, or if you weren't operating from a *should* or *must,* or if your attitude were more open and less judgmental, your problem would lessen or even disappear.

Praise

A common belief is that honest praise is helpful. Many authorities in the field of psychology endorse praise without reservation. Praise is supposed to build confidence, increase motivation and security, and stimulate productivity. However, what it is supposed to do and what it truly does are two different things.

What is praise? Praise is the expression of a favorable judgment that usually includes global adjectives, such as *nice, good,* and *wonderful.* However, praise is a judgment of a person, and people don't like to be judged. They feel uncomfortable when someone praises them because of the realization that praise is a judgment.

In an informal survey, 80 people were asked to state their feelings and thoughts about receiving praise. Most felt that praise had a negative and detrimental effect. They often felt a need to defend themselves against praise, as though they were protecting themselves from a threat. Feelings of embarrassment, bewilderment, anxiety, defensiveness, and resentment were often felt. People thought praise invited dependency and was nonconducive to self-reliance, self-direction, and self-control. Often, praise was heard and felt as flattery and as an insincere attempt to manipulate.

Although people have a natural need to feel they are wanted and that their efforts are appreciated, praise is probably not the best way to instill this feeling.

I-Rational Descriptive Feedback

Since praise has such detrimental effects, use the I-rational descriptive feedback instead. This technique will help you break the pattern of judgmental praise. It does not use global superlatives nor make judgment about the employee's personality and character. It is an explicit statement about the employee's behavior, achievement, or accomplishment.

Like the I-rational statements you learned in Chapter 7, it comes in three parts.

1. The first part is a clear, specific description of the employee's behavior or the result of that behavior. You accurately describe actual work or accomplishments. To assist yourself in describing it, ask yourself, "What is the employee doing or what has he or she done that I want to acknowledge?" Example: "The project covered each topic thoroughly and in the manner we discussed." On the other hand, "You're wonderful!" would be praise.

2. The second part calls for you to tell the employee how you feel or what you value about his or her behavior. Make certain that a nonjudgmental attitude is expressed nonverbally through your tone of voice, facial expression, gestures, and body posture. Example: "When you completed the project thoroughly in the manner we discussed, I felt relieved and satisfied."

3. The third part calls for you to state whether the employee's behavior has had a positive effect on the work or you. Example: "When you completed the project thoroughly in the manner we discussed, I felt relieved because the project deadline was met."

This method stresses what you value and provides specific, descriptive feedback to which the employee can relate.

Examples of I-Rational Descriptive Feedback

"I appreciated your working through lunch to type the Johnson report because the proposal might not have been considered if it had arrived late."

"By completing the ad layout the way the customer wanted it, you influenced him to sign the contract. Thanks!"

"I'm excited about the production record your group accomplished this month. Thank you."

This type of descriptive feedback fills the need of employees to feel wanted and appreciated, while not expressing it judgmentally. When employees experience your feedback as pleasing, the probability of their repeating the behavior is increased.

When you tell an employee specifically what he or she has done effectively, a special kind of pride is created. The natural response of most people is to be motivated to work even harder. People thrive on positive descriptive feedback. Too many supervisors don't give enough positive feedback. These supervisors "take for granted" a job well done. Too often employees who get their work done consistently without errors are overlooked.

TIPS FOR GIVING POSITIVE FEEDBACK

1. Maintain an evaluation program that provides objective, specific descriptive feedback on individual performance.

2. Recognize and stroke each employee according to his or her performance. Timing is significant: It's best to stroke promptly to carry the most impact.

3. Periodically review each position to determine how satisfying it is to the person filling it. Consider modifying a job to create more interest and challenge, especially if the employee has held it for a considerable time.

4. Consider job rotation to provide employees with a change of pace and variety.

5. Periodically review how each employee feels about salary, working conditions, job security, working relationships, company policy, and personal life. A lack of satisfaction in any of these areas can be demotivating.

6. Show appreciation for employees' contributions.

7. Periodically recheck goals, aspirations, and expectations as employees change their outlooks, interests, and career goals.

8. Keep employees up to date on the state of the business. A common demoralizing experience is for employees to find out from someone outside the business what is going on *in* the business.

SUMMARY

In this chapter, you learned why people have difficulty receiving positive feedback, ways to receive and give positive feedback, and the advantages of positive feedback for productivity and performance.

The fundamental need for recognition was covered. You found that two mottos—"What you stroke is what you get" and "Negative strokes are better than none"—are important to keep in mind when giving positive feedback. You learned that praise has negative consequences, while positive, specific, descriptive feedback about accomplishments has positive consequences.

11 Payoffs for Success

He who gains a victory over other men is strong; but he who gains a victory over himself is all powerful.

Lao-Tse

Not everything that is faced can be changed easily, but nothing can be changed until it is faced.

James Baldwin

According to a *Time* magazine survey, only 3 percent of the U.S. public write down their goals, 10 percent have strong goals committed to memory, 50 percent have short-range goals only, and 37 percent have hardly any goals at all. Which category do you fit into? The answer will strongly influence how successful you will be at putting into practice the techniques and ideas covered in this book. Whatever your choice, it is important to be aware that you alone are responsible for the consequences. Accepting them is a crucial ingredient for professional development.

As you read this book and completed the various exercises, you learned labels for what you already do that does and doesn't work well, along with exercises to deal with those areas that needed improvement. You learned new approaches you can use on the job and became more aware of things you would like to stop. In other words, you now have the opportunity to choose the behaviors you want to continue, start, or improve on.

In summary, you learned that assertion on the job involves the following elements:

1. *An active orientation.* It is important to think through your work goals, the steps necessary to achieve them, and how you can utilize your talents to the fullest possible extent.

2. *Ability to do the job.* Obstacles sometimes arise in work because you have not mastered the skills you need for your particular job. It's important to identify what is causing those obstacles. Determining the underlying cause is essential because habits such as poor discipline, poor organization, and poor concentration often cause loss of control of self and others.

3. *Ability to be in charge of your anxieties and fears.* Tensions can produce fatigue, irritability, and poor judgment. Fear of a specific work situation may lead to avoidance of the very task needed to get your job done and to keep you from achieving your work goals. You can reach personal power by self-management and directing your life. Reread Chapter 4 on building self-esteem. Work on incorporating those essential characteristics on page 72. Create a support system of family, friends, and peers who are good listeners, nonjudgmental, and willing to take the time to sit down with you to discuss what's bothering you.

4. *Good interpersonal relations on the job.* An important aspect of your job is being able to relate to peers, employees, and supervisors, to make requests and ask favors, to say no when necessary, and to handle putdowns.

5. *Ability to negotiate the system.* This requires a knowledge of the culture of the organization and the specific skills that will enable you to work within, through, or against it to achieve your goals.

Keeping these assertive elements in mind and following through on them will assist you in using the assertive supervisory style with success.

SELF-MOTIVATION

One way to enhance your success on the job is to be aware of how your expectations and habits lead to self-motivating or self-defeating behaviors. The following story illustrates this point. Norman Vincent Peale told of a group of people who, at the end of one year, wrote down their expectations for the coming year. Each sealed the "new year's expectations" in an envelope to be opened and read aloud at the end of the following year. The results were worthy of note.

One man had written, "In the next year, all that I can expect is more of the old, miserable same." That's exactly what he got.

A woman had listed ten worthy goals she expected to reach. Nine of the ten had come to fruition.

Another man, basing his expectations on the characteristics of Capricorn, his birth sign, predicted, "I look for difficulty and frustration." He got them, too.

One woman in the group, whose birth sign was the same, not knowing she should expect difficulties and not having predicted them, enjoyed a rewarding year.

One man in the group died during the year. When the envelope was opened, his "expectation" read: "As none of the men in my family have survived beyond the age of sixty, therefore, I expect to die this year." and he did—one month before his sixtieth birthday.

Each of you, whether or not you will admit it, will receive what you expect, either positive or negative.

Everyone has a self-taught cycle like the one shown in Figure 11.1.

You can go in one direction or another, either positively or negatively. Negative self-talk can cause failure and can interfere with your ability to use the assertive approach.

Motivation starts with your beliefs. You have a belief pattern scale that looks something like this:

Constructive Belief Patterns	Restrictive Belief Patterns
+	−
Desire	Fear-compulsive
"I choose to" attitude	"I have to"
"I've decided to do it!"	"I can't do it!"

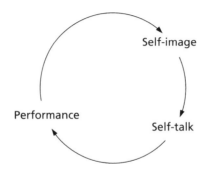

FIGURE 11.1

The self-taught cycle.

You learned that the conditioning process has a significant influence on your present behavior. Conversely, creative ability can be developed as well. In each person's brain are stored 10 trillion pieces of information to call upon. William James said a person uses 10 percent of his or her potential; modern scientists say 2 percent. Everything that has ever happened to you or to any human being is stored in some way in the central nervous system. Everything you have seen, felt, or experienced in any way is retained. This total accumulation of experiences, knowledge, and training is called *potential*. And your effectiveness is your ability to use your potential.

The learning process for any behavior pattern is in three steps: desire, the acquisition of knowledge, and repetition. You change a negative or restrictive habit to a positive, constructive habit simply by starting on the first step of the learning process.

1. *Develop an ardent desire.* Desiring results for a given period of time with positive expectations will force you to enter situations without recognizing the possibility of defeat, to look to each day as an opportunity to earn and justify your rewards, to develop the habits of success necessary for great achievement, to expect tremendous dividends because you have already made the proper investments, and to seek a challenge to reach your potential.

2. *Acquire knowledge.* The information in this book can be used to internalize new and more effective methods to be successful.

   Think of your mind as a data computer. What you put into your brain, what you vividly imagine in a clear, concise way is what you become! We cannot break the law of the universe that we "tend to draw to ourselves that which we send out from ourselves," that no people can attract things to themselves while their thoughts repel them. It is important to understand that the human tendency to become precisely what you imagine yourself to be is a vital ingredient for self-improvement. Whatever you picture and hold in your mind continually tends to come to you.

   You can mentally rehearse doing a positive, constructive activity. You can project yourself in the future already doing what you want to do or being what you want to be. The best formula is to draw on successful experiences or instances when you do this.

3. *Repeat the new behavior.* By thinking positive thoughts repeatedly, by talking constructively of and to yourself over and over again, you can slowly and finally become that which you would like to be.

Remember, whatever we vividly imagine, ardently desire, sincerely believe, and enthusiastically act upon will inevitably come to pass.

You might be surprised to know that the brain doesn't know the difference between visualizing something inside your head or acting it out externally! This means you can visualize yourself being successful and assertive in a given situation as often as you want. The brain doesn't know the difference or care!

Keep in mind that life is a classroom. You choose various situations and relationships to grow and develop . . . to learn lessons and pass tests on them. This school of life is similar to going to school. Each grade offered you certain lessons and tests to pass. When you got good grades on those lessons, you were promoted to the next grade with a different series of lessons and tests to pass. One of the reasons that each person is so unique is that each has different lessons to learn and tests to pass.

Some people are in kindergarten, some in grammar school, others in high school or college. Then there were those masters that walked the planet to show how it is really done!

EXERCISE 11.1 | **Systematic Assertive Procedures**

A method that can help you reach your goal of being an assertive supervisor is the procedure outlined here. Think of a situation with which you have been having difficulty. Analyze this situation by responding to the following questions.

1. Clarify the situation you want to handle more effectively: What is my goal? What do I want?

2. How will assertive behavior on my part help me to accomplish my goal?

3. What would I usually do to avoid asserting myself in this situation?

4. What do I want to give up that will help me assert myself?

5. What might be stopping me from asserting myself?

6. Am I anxious about asserting myself?

7. What are my rights in this situation?

8. Have I done my homework? Do I have the information I need to go ahead and act? If not, where can I get it?

9. How will I:
   Let the other person know I hear and understand him or her?

   Let the other person know how I feel?

   Tell him or her what I want?

10. When I talk to the other person, I want to:
    - Pick an appropriate time and setting.
    - Affirm any positive action the person has taken, no matter how small.
    - Focus on incongruent behavior (do the words and nonverbal behavior match?).
    - Use "I" messages rather than "you" messages.
    - Use empathetic listening: Hear the other person out, and restate or paraphrase what I think I hear him or her say before stating my own views.

Use this format each time you want to examine a problem and arrive at an approach for handling it. You'll discover that after you've used this system on two or three occasions, you will be able to apply the process quickly and with ease.

THE CHANGE PROCESS*

Modifying and improving your behavior can be exciting and discouraging at the same time. You often expect change to happen immediately, and, if it doesn't, you believe it works for others but not yourself. In this book, you have completed several exercises that will improve your ability to behave assertively. How quickly you will internalize the assertive style will be determined partly by your beliefs about change. Some people choose to believe that change is hard and difficult. As a result, that's exactly the way change is for them.

People often resist change because they are uncertain as to the results they will get. However, knowing how the change works and having a better understanding of its dynamics will enable you to approach change more positively. The following model consists of a four-step process for integrating and internalizing a new behavior or skill so that the behavior or skill eventually becomes part of your behavior pattern for improved effectiveness.

CHANGE PROCESS MODEL

Step I Nonawareness	Step II Awareness	Step III Internalizing	Step IV Integration
UNCONSCIOUS of one's behavior that results in ineffectiveness	CONSCIOUS of one's behavior that results in ineffectiveness	CONSCIOUSLY putting into practice the new behavior or skill	UNCON-SCIOUSLY applying the new behavior or skill

---

*This "change process" originally appeared in my book *Listening: The Forgotten Skill* (New York, John Wiley and Sons, 1982).

INTERNAL EXPERIENCE THAT TAKES PLACE WHEN INTEGRATING A NEW SKILL OR BEHAVIOR

Resistance: Natural tendency to stay with what is familiar.

Being unsure: Feeling phoney when starting to apply new skills and behaviors.

Assimilation: Feeling less phoney and becoming comfortable with the new behavior and new skill.

Transference: Applying behavior or skills learned in one setting over to another setting or situation.

Integration: Automatically and unconsciously reproducing the new behavior or skill as a natural part of you.

A major part of this change process is letting others know that you are going to be somewhat different. People like to be able to predict how you will behave. They feel uncomfortable, even threatened, when they aren't able to predict accurately. You will decrease their discomfort by discussing with them what you have become aware of that you want to modify. (I have found I could even request their support, and get it!) The main point here is to plan your change so that your change will be gradual. This usually results in a series of small successes. If you take a "giant leap," it might overwhelm the other person, resulting in an unsuccessful outcome.

AUTHOR'S FINAL THOUGHT

I have learned a great deal by writing this book. Writing it has given me the opportunity to be more clear on how to share information in written form as well as other communication media. It is similar to conducting seminars but more precise and thorough. I'm not sure who values most from a relationship where there is a "sharer" and a "sharee." My guess is it will be the one most open to new ideas and change. Thank you for reading this book.

The future does not belong to those who are content with today . . . rather it will belong to those who will blend vision, reason, and courage in a personal commitment.
Robert F. Kennedy

People cannot discover new oceans unless they have the courage to lose sight of the shore.
Unknown

Bibliography

Alberti, Robert E., and Emmons, Michael L., *Stand Up, Speak Out, Talk Back! The Key to Self-Assertive Behavior*, New York: Pocket Books, 1975.

Alberti, Robert E., and Emmons, Michael L., *Your Perfect Right: A Guide to Assertive Behavior*, San Luis Obispo, CA: Impact, 1970.

Antany, Jay, *Management and Machiavelli*, San Diego, CA: Pfeiffer & Co., 1994.

Autry, James, *Life and Work, A Manager's Search for Meaning*, New York: William Morrow & Co., 1994.

Bittle, Lester R., *What Every Supervisor Should Know*, New York: McGraw-Hill, 1974.

Bramson, Robert M., Ph.D., *Coping with Difficult People*, New York: Anchor Press/Doubleday, 1991.

Brothers, Joyce, *Positive Plus*, New York: G. P. Putnam's Sons, 1994.

Bryce, Sheradon, *Joy Riding the Universe*, Salt Lake City, UT: HomeWords Publishing, 1993.

Burley-Allen, Madelyn, "How to Build a Better You: Starting Now," *Listening for Happiness*, Fairfield, CA: Showcase, 1981.

Burley-Allen, Madelyn, *Listening: The Forgotten Skill*, Second Edition, New York: John Wiley & Sons, 1995.

Coonradt, Charles A., with Nelson, Lee, *The Game of Work*, Salt Lake City, UT: Shadow Mountain, 1991.

Dyer, Wayne D., Dr., *Real Magic*, New York: Harper Collins, 1992.

Ellis, Albert, and Harper, Robert A., *A Guide to Rational Living*, Los Angeles: Melvin Powers, Wilshire Book Co., 1975, 1961.

Fersterheim, Herbert, and Baer, Jean, *Don't Say Yes When You Want to Say No: How Assertiveness Training Can Change Your Life*, New York: David McKay, 1975.

Fink, Darley Diana, Tate, John T., and Rose, Michael D., *Speedreading*, New York: John Wiley & Sons, 1982.

Fuller, R. Buckminster, *Critical Path*, New York: St. Martin's Press, 1981.

Horney, Karen, M.D., *Neurosis and Human Growth*, New York: W.W. Norton, 1950.

Jongeward, Dorothy, and James, Muriel, *Born to Win*, Reading, MA: Addison-Wesley, 1975.

Laborde, Genie Z., *Influencing with Integrity*, Palo Alto, CA: Syntony Publishers, 1987.

Meninger, Jut, *Success Through Transactional Analysis*, New York: Grosset and Dunlap, 1973.

Moyers, Bill, *Healing and the Mind*, New York: Doubleday, 1993.

Peters, Tom, *Liberation Management*, New York: Fawcett Columbine, 1992.

Phelps, Stanless, and Austin, Nancy, *The Assertive Woman*, San Luis Obispo, CA: Impact, 1975.

Prukop, John R. (Chairman), *Citizens Rule Book, We the People Committee*, 11910-C Meridian E., Suite 142, Puyallup, WA 98373, 1971.

Rajneesh, Bhagwan Shree, *And the Flowers Showered*, Poona, India: A Rajneesh Foundation Publication, 1975.

Smigel, Lloyd, *Handle with Care*, Oceanside, CA: Smigel Publishing, 1993.

Stedman, W. David, Lavaugh, G. Lewis, (Edited by), *Our Ageless Constitution*, Evanston, IL: United Communications of America, Inc., 1987.

Index